The IRS

The People

TIME FOR REAL TAX REFORM

Edited by

Jack Kemp

and

Ken Blackwell

The Heritage Foundation
214 Massachusetts Avenue, N.E.
Washington, D.C. 20002
1-202-546-4400
www.heritage.org

ISBN 0-89195-077-X

TABLE OF CONTENTS

ACKNOWLEDGMENTS

A project of this magnitude is never possible without the contributions of many people. The authors, of course, deserve special thanks. The time and energy they devoted to their chapters were driven by a belief in a better future for ordinary and hard-working Americans. Their selflessness in promoting a fair and simple pro-growth tax system should be an inspiration to all of us. We also gratefully acknowledge Rush Limbaugh's thoughtful foreword.

The staff of The Heritage Foundation deserves special thanks. Under Edwin J. Feulner's leadership, Heritage constantly reminds us that principles do matter and that policymakers should strive to achieve the ideal. We thank Daniel J. Mitchell for conceiving of this easy-to-read but important guide to tax reform, as well as Stuart M. Butler, Vice President for Domestic and Economic Policy Studies, and Angela Antonelli, Director of the Thomas A. Roe Institute for Economic Policy Studies, for helping to ensure that this book became a reality.

Most of all, we should thank the people behind the scenes. John Barry of America's Future Foundation and Amy Holmes of the Independent Women's Forum provided invaluable research assistance. At The Heritage Foundation, we especially thank Managing Editor Janice A. Smith and Senior Editor Richard Odermatt for their oversight and editing talents, and Administrative Assistant Jennifer Olsen for cheerfully taking care of details. We also thank the capable staff of Heritage's Publishing Services Department, who turned these chapters into this book: Ann Klucsarits, Director; William T. Poole, Copy Editor; Michelle Smith, Design and Publishing Coordinator; and Thomas J. Timmons, Manager of Graphic Design Services.

Rush Limbaugh, host of the highest-rated national radio talk show in America, began his career in broadcasting part-time, at age 16, in his hometown of Cape Girardeau, Missouri. With only a break to work for the Kansas City Royals, he has informed and entertained America over the airwaves for more than 30 years. Today, his calls for commonsense policies–especially tax reform–are broadcast daily from New York over the Excellence in Broadcasting Network, which is carried by 600 radio stations and heard by 20 million people weekly. Mr. Limbaugh, who was inducted into the Radio Hall of Fame in November 1993, has been profiled on CBS's "60 Minutes" and ABC's "20/20," and in numerous publications, including *US News & World Report*, *National Review*, *Time*, and *USA Today*. The 1992 and 1995 recipient of the Marconi Award for Syndicated Radio Personality of the Year, he was inducted into the National Association of Broadcasters Hall of Fame in April 1998. His two best-selling books, *The Way Things Ought to Be* and *See, I Told You So*, have sold nearly 9 million copies.

FOREWORD

The Internal Revenue Code is immoral, punitive, and un-American.

America is a constitutional republic founded on the premise of individual liberty. Our Founding Fathers created a beacon of freedom, a nation where government was to be the servant of the people, not the master. Unlike the rigid societies of Europe, the United States was designed to be a land of opportunity, a Mecca of upward mobility that allows the lowest-born to rise as far and as fast as their ability and hard work will take them.

But is this really the case anymore? Because of our nation's tradition of free markets and entrepreneurship, we recoil at the notion that Americans exist to sweat and toil and work for the government. According to the Tax Foundation, taxes now consume 38 percent of the average family's budget. This is more than they pay for food, clothing, housing, and transportation put together.

Paul Craig Roberts, who served in Ronald Reagan's Treasury Department, points out that medieval serfs were considered slaves, yet they had to pay only one-third of their income in taxes. We may not be slaves yet, but the incrementalism of class envy over the past 50 years has reached into the deepest foundations of society. This is not what the Founders of this nation had in mind.

The government should exist for the people. Our representatives should be answerable to us. We should not serve them. We don't work for our neighbors. We don't work for the government. We work for our families and ourselves. Our tax system should mirror these values. It should be based on the Constitution's promise of equal treatment. This means taxes should be low. It means the tax rate should be the same, no matter how much you earn. And it means that politicians should not seize our wealth.

Tragically, too many people in this country have accepted the notion, promulgated by liberals, that all wealth belongs to the government: What you have is what Washington permits you to keep. It's your allowance, so to speak. This is dangerous nonsense. The fact that there are a lot of people who think such radical confiscation is okay is an indication of just how successful the brainwashing has been.

And who in our society are the targets of confiscation? The producers. The achievers. The people who work hard and save money. The people who take care of their families. The people who do the right thing. Those are the people under assault. They are the ones under attack. We are victimizing the people who are paying for all the services this country provides. A virulent class envy has taken hold.

Yet some think it is perfectly fine to punish the rich. Little do they realize that they may be talking about themselves. Back in 1997, when the liberals were attacking the capital gains tax cut, they said most of the benefits would go to the top 20 percent. What they didn't tell you is that the top 20 percent included any taxpayer with income above $56,200. The so-called rich include a lot of hard-working, middle-class families who save and invest, because if you build a nest egg for your retirement or your kids, you're rich.

Do you think income redistribution is a proper role for government in a free society? I don't. I invite you to try to change my mind. I warn you in advance, you will fail. Because I'm right, and you're wrong. But I have compassion and hope in my heart for you—I will do everything I can to get you aligned on the correct side. If there has been anything that has motivated me to get behind a microphone, it is taxes and what is happening to people of this country because of IRS oppression. Too many of you have been duped, brainwashed into accepting some notions that are frankly un-American, and I mean that in the greatest sense of the phrase.

One such notion that has always amazed me is what happens when hard-working people express a desire to keep more of what they've earned by saying they want a tax cut. Or when they say they want our wretched tax code replaced with a flat tax, or even a national sales tax. What happens to those people? They are accused of being greedy. They are accused of being selfish, cold-hearted, mean-spirited, and unwilling to share.

But do you know where the real greed is in America? Government. Every time a tax cut is proposed, defenders of government confiscation cry out almost in unison, demanding: "But how are we going to pay for it?" Any time tax reform becomes an issue, the same knee-jerk response is repeated. But when the same agents of confiscation in the federal government decide to raise your taxes, they have no concern at all about how you are going to pay for it. There is more greed and selfishness and insatiable demand in the federal government than you will ever find in the entire private sector.

There's nothing that brings foam to a liberal's mouth quite like the prospect of tax cuts and tax reform. Vice President Al Gore constantly calls tax cut proposals "risky schemes." When Congress moved to cut capital gains and estate taxes in 1997, *The New York Times* angrily editorialized against "tricky provisions," shrieking that these would be "showering the rich with benefits." Lawrence Summers, Bill Clinton's Deputy Treasury Secretary, could not contain himself when death tax reform began to gain momentum in Congress. He actually stated that "There is no case other than selfishness."

What is really amazing is that the Left does not hide its agenda. Witness an article in *The New York Times* which casually points out that the estate tax is levied "both as a means of raising revenue and as a way to limit the concentration of wealth." Defenders of the estate tax openly acknowledge that this burden is for the express purpose of redistribution of wealth. And you may think Karl Marx was the one who stated, "you have to raise revenue somewhere, and ability to pay is the right principle for doing it," but it was Larry Summers from the Clinton Treasury Department. Translation: "We, your federal overseers, are entitled to your money; and the more you have, the more we'll take. If you don't like it, you must be an anarchist."

So there you have it. Although figures from the Administration's own budget reveal that Bill Clinton has taken more of your income in confiscatory taxation than any other President in history, you are selfish if you believe that tax relief—of any kind—is in order. And if you actually have the gall to want a flat tax or something like that, well, you must be some sort of robber baron who eats poor people for breakfast.

Let me tell you something: The Left's primary motivation for soak-the-rich taxes is not money. The death tax and the capital gains tax together have never raised more than a tiny percentage of total federal revenues. These two taxes have existed only to punish achievers. These two taxes are based on resentment. This is why liberals don't want tax cuts. This is why they don't want tax reform. The hate-and-envy crowd wants to punish success.

Not that they mind spending our money. Oppressive and complicated taxes increase the power and influence of the political class. Even better, the money that is raised is used to create more dependency among the population. It is going out to some constituency to empower a politician. This is social engineering operating under the cover of the federal tax code.

Of all the idiotic provisions in the tax code, the death tax may be the worst one. Small business owners, farmers, and entrepreneurs find themselves in Washington's sights, having to fight to protect what they've built over a lifetime of work. The tax is confiscatory, and it is double taxation of the worst kind. It is the sort of thing that makes me want to shout from the rooftops, "Washington, it's not your money!"

Interestingly enough, the death tax raises just 1.2 percent of federal revenues—hitting the estates of only 37,000 people, less than 2 percent of those who die each year. Most of the rich are able to maintain their "concentration of wealth" despite Washington's grasping fingers—with good estate planning advice from their tax lawyers.

If liberals were smart, they would get rid of the estate tax. That way, rich people would stop hiding their money, fire their accountants and tax lawyers, and simply concentrate on creating more wealth. The only problem, at least from a left-wing perspective, is that this takes away a chance to demagogue. It was Bill Clinton, after all, who said, "We cannot put our prosperity at risk with time-bomb tax cuts." But the only things that risk being exploded here are the lies of this Administration.

This is America! If somebody has a lot of money when they die, he or she ought to have the freedom to do whatever they want with whatever they've earned. The IRS should not come in at the time of death and say, "All right, 60 percent of it is ours." What bothers me more, however, is that some people defend this type of legalized theft. That frightens and depresses me.

It could never happen if the economic and history education in this country were not so woefully inept. None of this class-warfare nonsense would get past first base if there were genuine, sufficient education in this country about wealth, about hard work, about achievement. The whole concept that, at death, your money is no longer yours ought to outrage everybody. And the fact that it doesn't is a real eye-opener.

If you want to argue that citizens ought not be able to inherit their wealth and ought not be able to pass it on, that it ought to go into the redistributionists' coffers, please be advised that you are articulating (perhaps unbeknownst to you) socialist dogma. But I am a conservative, and I believe that it is not the role of a handful of politicians and unelected IRS bureaucrats to determine whether parents should be free to leave their wealth to their children rather than to the government. As a conservative, I believe that it is the people who earn the money who have the right to decide what to do with it—not the government.

America is at a crossroads. Our tax burden has climbed to record levels, and the Left is hoping you will behave like sheep and be sheared without protest. And if they can get away with this, they will come back for more. Senate Minority Leader Tom Daschle (D–SD) has said: "We have the lowest tax rate of any industrialized country in the world. Our view is that we've got to make the tax system more fair [translation: raise your taxes]. But certainly, I don't think that many people are overtaxed."

The other alternative—the one I desperately hope will occur—is that the American people reclaim their freedom. That taxpayers rise up in revolt and demand tax cuts. That we scrap the IRS and replace the tax code with a simple and fair system that imposes only one tax rate.

The number of people who are actually opposed to a tax cut—if you believe the polls—is a sure sign of how ignorant so many Americans have been made, on purpose. It would break the Founders' hearts. They would say, "For all we went through, you modern Americans don't even take the time to preserve your liberty. You don't remember our sacrifice and struggle that gave you this opportunity—and you don't even cherish the sacred trust that protects your freedom."

America's heritage is its greatness. Our nation began because of a thirst for freedom that was so great that ordinary citizens took up arms to wrest independence from the superpower of that time. We conquered the frontier and built a prosperous economy. We defeated totalitarianism in World War II and, thanks to the greatness of Ronald Reagan, vanquished communism without firing a shot. We stand alone as the only country of consequence to pay lip service, at least, to freedom and capitalism.

But what will the future hold? Will we have a tax code that reflects the values of independence and entrepreneurship? Or will we fall victim to the narrow-minded resentment of class warfare? The answer will determine the kind of nation we leave for our children and grandchildren.

RUSH LIMBAUGH

Jack Kemp is co-director of Empower America, a public policy and advocacy organization that he founded in 1993 with former U.S. Secretary of Education and National Drug Control Policy Director William J. Bennett, Ambassador Jeane Kirkpatrick, and former Congressman Vin Weber. Mr. Kemp was nominated to be the Republican Party's candidate for Vice President in August 1996. Previously, he served as Chairman of the National Commission on Economic Growth and Tax Reform, a congressional commission tasked with studying how restructuring the tax code would unleash the entrepreneurial spirit of Americans and promote economic growth. Before serving in the Reagan Administration as HUD Secretary, he served in the U.S. House of Representatives for 18 years, which included seven years as Chairman of the House Republican Leadership Conference. Mr. Kemp received his B.A. from Occidental College in California.

J. Kenneth Blackwell is Ohio's Secretary of State. In 1994, Mr. Blackwell was appointed and subsequently elected State Treasurer. He served as the co-chairman of the U.S. Census Monitoring Board. In 1997, he served on the U.S. Department of Labor's Advisory Council on Employee Welfare and Pension Benefit Plans. He also served on the Board of Directors of the National Taxpayers Union. In 1995, the Majority Leader of the U.S. Senate and Speaker of the U.S. House of Representatives appointed Mr. Blackwell to the National Commission on Economic Growth and Tax Reform. In 1989, President Bush appointed him Undersecretary of the U.S. Department of Housing and Urban Development. First elected to public office in 1977, Mr. Blackwell served as Vice Mayor for the City of Cincinnati and then was elected Mayor in 1980. He received his B.S. and M.Ed. degrees from Xavier University.

INTRODUCTION

In 1995, we were asked by Speaker of the House Newt Gingrich and Senate Majority Leader Bob Dole to organize a commission that would address the problems associated with the current income tax code. Working with some of the most diligent and thoughtful people in America, the National Commission on Economic Growth and Tax Reform concluded that the tax code suffers from three principal defects: First, it is economically destructive, destroying jobs, penalizing savings and investment, and punishing personal effort. Second, it is impossibly complex. And third, it is overly intrusive, allowing the Internal Revenue Service to infringe upon our privacy and personal freedoms.

The commission's common-sense approach was to design a pro-growth, pro-family tax system for the 21st century. Our recommendations were simple: Economic growth, the engine of opportunity and prosperity, can be unleashed only by a tax code that encourages initiative, hard work, and saving. Any new system must be based on fairness and simplicity.

When The Heritage Foundation asked us to edit this volume on tax reform, we were delighted, because it continues this incredibly important effort to free the American spirit of entrepreneurialism and individual private enterprise. Compiling a book for all Americans—not just politicians—on the need for tax reform was a simple and natural next step, because almost every adult American has experienced the fear and uncertainty that comes with filing their annual tax returns.

Every taxpayer understands that the Internal Revenue Code is unfair. Every taxpayer recognizes that the tax code is anti-growth, penalizing the behaviors that would add wealth to our economy. By wide margins, people want the current system reformed. Many want it scrapped.

The interesting question is, of course, what should take its place? Should we enact a flat tax? And if we do, should it be the "pure" version popularized by House Majority Leader Richard Armey (R–TX), Senator Richard Shelby (R–AL), and presidential candidate Steve Forbes? Some even think we should repeal the Sixteenth Amendment to the Constitution and replace the income tax with a national sales tax.

One thing is clear: Doing nothing is not an option. Retaining today's income tax will mean retaining the Internal Revenue Service and a tax code that entails 569 forms, 17,000 pages of fine-print law and regulations, and 100,000-plus IRS personnel. Doing nothing means that special-interest groups will continue to manipulate the system to their advantage. The status quo is a recipe for corruption, despair, and discrimination.

This book, then, is a guide to the key issues surrounding tax reform, the problems with today's tax code, and the best solutions to those problems. Written in a user-friendly style, it does not use the special jargon of "inside-the-beltway" tax lobbyists. Instead, ideas are presented honestly and discussed fairly in a way that all Americans can understand.

As many of the authors explain, the flat tax is an extremely popular solution to today's tax problems. In part, this is because the flat tax is something Americans can understand, unlike the current system. A flat tax, quite simply, will tax all income once and at one low rate. Perhaps best of all, the flat tax is fair, ensuring that the rich and powerful play by the same rules as the rest of us.

It should be noted that, even though economists like the flat tax because it will boost job creation and increase savings and investment, this book is not about gross domestic product, capital formation, or macroeconomic policy. To be sure, many of the authors explain why a low-rate tax system will encourage work, risk-taking, and entrepreneurship. There also is some discussion of the beneficial impact on wages and growth when the bias against savings and investment is eliminated. These things are important; we all want more opportunity and prosperity for our children. But this book takes a broader view, building on the pro-growth, pro-family recommendations of the Tax Reform Commission.

Many of the chapters, for instance, focus on important moral and philosophical issues associated with tax reform: What is a fair tax system? Is it possible to have a tax code that treats everyone equally? How will tax reform affect ordinary people? Can we strip the IRS of its abusive powers? Will tax reform be good for families, middle-class Americans, women, farmers, and small business owners?

The book begins with Herman Cain's inspiring call for economic opportunity and analysis of why a flat tax will make the American dream more accessible to all. President of the National Restaurant Association, Herman uses his own fascinating life story to personalize the importance of upward mobility. Most significantly, he explains how the ability to get ahead in life is restricted today by provisions in the tax code that are designed to punish those who achieve prosperity based on their own hard work.

Former Senator Malcolm Wallop builds on this discussion with an insider's view of how the current tax system undermines the values of all involved and breeds corruption. Having served on the tax-writing committee in Congress, Senator Wallop is well aware of how legislators are encouraged to bend the system and curry favor, how the IRS is encouraged to abuse its powers, and how taxpayers are motivated to evade the heavy burden the code imposes on them.

Richard Rahn, Senior Fellow at the Discovery Institute and former Vice President and chief economist of the United States

Chamber of Commerce, gives us a closer look at everyone's least favorite part of the government—the IRS. After highlighting the abusive nature of tax collecting, he offers a relatively optimistic assessment that technological changes will force policymakers to reform the tax code—not necessarily because they want to do the right thing, but because the tax collection system will collapse because of widespread evasion if they do not.

The next chapter examines why small businesses are penalized especially heavily by the Internal Revenue Code. Jack Faris, President of the National Federation of Independent Business, argues that scrapping the tax code is the only way to promote real reform. He explains why NFIB is promoting a movement to "Scrap the Code." And although many of his arguments are made within the context of how the Internal Revenue Code is bad for small business, they are just as relevant for individual taxpayers, especially those who wish to follow Herman Cain's example and achieve the American dream by becoming entrepreneurs.

Next, Doug Bandow of the Cato Institute analyzes a broader issue: the morality of the tax code. He examines the philosophical and religious roots of equality before the law and shows how our heritage, based on Judeo-Christian principles, establishes clearly that a just law must apply equally to all citizens. The implication, needless to say, is that it is discriminatory for the government to impose special penalties on some taxpayers while granting special favors to others.

Daniel J. Mitchell, McKenna Senior Fellow in Political Economy at The Heritage Foundation, builds on the discussion of equality by explaining how the flat tax satisfies the principles of simplicity and fairness. He explains exactly how a tax that taxes all income one time and at one low rate would work; he shows us how simple it is—with only two tax forms—and discusses the features and benefits of the flat tax that make it the best-known and most popular of the reform proposals under consideration today.

The next four chapters offer clear explanations of why a flat tax will be good for various sectors of the country. First, Randy Tate, Executive Director of the Christian Coalition, argues forcefully that the flat tax will be good news for the middle class and calls on policymakers to guarantee this by making sure that the flat tax has the lowest possible rate. Setting the rate at 20 percent or below ensures that the vast majority of taxpayers will get to keep more of the money they earn. Combined with the fact that a flat tax will increase opportunity and economic growth, this means more security for almost every American.

Next comes an analysis of how the current code hurts families and how a flat tax will benefit them. It is written by Mike Farris, head of the Home School Legal Defense Foundation, who fights for families on a daily basis. In this chapter, he turns his talents to tax policy, arguing how the current system especially penalizes married couples and large families. More important, he shows how a flat tax will end these preposterous penalties and give families more control over their own destinies.

In a thoughtful discussion of women's advances over the past 60 years, Linda Chavez of the Center for Equal Opportunity explains that, rather than making life better for women, the current system makes life harder for them. Women who want to devote time to their children often are forced into the job market because excessive taxation makes it harder for their families to get by on just one income, but thanks to such provisions as the marriage penalty, the tax code punishes career women as well. Linda explains how the flat tax will end these perverse forms of social engineering and give women—more than ever an economic force in America—more freedom to choose what is best for them.

Another group that is victimized by the current tax code is made up of farmers and ranchers. Like other small business people, they are affected adversely by high tax rates and the complexity of the code. But, as American Farm Bureau Federation President Dean Kleckner points out, they also are hit particularly hard by capital gains taxes and death taxes. And because farmers and ranchers often are land-rich but cash-poor, such taxes can be the death of the family farm. Dean explains how tax reform will get rid of these destructive forms of double taxation.

In the next two chapters, we take the reader into more politically sensitive issues facing tax reformers–specifically, the loss of itemized deductions.

Elaine L. Chao uses her insights as a former President of United Way to explore whether charities will win or lose under a flat tax without the charitable contributions deduction. She finds that Americans donate more when they have more income. And since a flat tax is certain to increase income and boost wealth, this will be particularly good news for churches and human service organizations.

Bruce Bartlett, a former Reagan Administration appointee at the U.S. Treasury, then analyzes how the flat tax and the loss of the mortgage interest deduction will affect the housing market. He reviews the evidence and finds that tax reform will be good news for homeowners, homebuilders, and realtors.

We have included a thorough discussion of a national sales tax, the other prominent reform being discussed today. Written by David Burton, former head of tax policy for the U.S. Chamber of Commerce, this chapter explains how a national sales tax would operate and the benefits it would generate for the economy. Much of this material will seem familiar, and with good reason. Both a flat tax and a national sales tax are single-rate taxes that eliminate double taxation of savings and investment. It therefore should come as no surprise that both plans would produce similar benefits.

The final issue that must be discussed is how tax reforms, once achieved, can be protected from the machinations of future politicians. Grover Norquist, President of Americans for Tax Reform, shows why requiring a "supermajority" vote to raise taxes is a proven way to control taxes and spending. Simply stated, if future increases in the tax rate can be enacted only by a two-thirds vote of Congress, the rate is more likely to remain low and fair.

In the concluding chapter, Dan Mitchell summarizes why tax reform–and especially repealing the current code and implementing the flat tax–truly promises the American people a brighter future. The tax code can be fair, honest, and simple. Under a flat tax or a similar pro-growth system, politicians no longer would be able to micromanage the economy or to bully us with their social engineering. Instead, we would have a tax code that rewards us by creating jobs, expanding opportunity, and building wealth.

We sincerely hope you enjoy this book. Never before have so many real-world experts come together to offer such user-friendly information on tax reform. We encourage you to share this knowledge with your friends, neighbors, and coworkers.

Tax reform will not happen unless you and other citizens decide that it is going to happen. So spread the news, and let's build a nationwide grassroots movement committed to simplicity and fairness. Only when we unite can the special interests in Washington be vanquished.

As Abraham Lincoln once remarked, "with public sentiment, nothing can fail; without it, nothing can succeed."

The Honorable Jack Kemp
Co-Director, Empower America

J. Kenneth Blackwell
Secretary of State of Ohio

Herman Cain, one of *Ebony* magazine's 100 Most Influential Black Americans in 1997, is CEO and President of the National Restaurant Association. Following service in the Navy and work at the Coca-Cola Company, he joined the Pillsbury Company in 1977. He was named Vice President and General Manager for the Philadelphia region after nine months with the Burger King Corporation, a subsidiary of Pillsbury. In 1986, Mr. Cain was selected to assume the presidency of the declining Godfather's Pizza subsidiary; two years later, he successfully led an effort by a senior management group to purchase the chain from Pillsbury, and subsequently made it a success. The recipient of the 1996 Horatio Alger Award, Mr. Cain received a B.S. in mathematics from Morehouse College and an M.S. in computer science from Purdue University.

1

RESTORING THE AMERICAN DREAM

Herman Cain
CEO and President,
National Restaurant Association

America's income tax code is broken, and no amount of tinkering around the edges is going to fix it. For starters, it is too complicated. My 102-year-old grandmother, who is 16 years older than the tax code, would describe what we have now as a 7 million-word mess. I would not want to get her started on the 17,000 pages of laws and regulations put out by the Internal Revenue Service (IRS) or the 8 billion pages of forms and instructions it sends out every year.

The tax code is more than too complicated, however; it is unfair as well. High tax rates punish success. Those high rates also mean that deductions, exemptions, and credits are more valuable to the wealthy than they are to those in the lower tax brackets. The unvarnished truth is that the tax code is a chain around the throat of the poor. It constrains people at the lowest economic level and prevents them from joining the economic mainstream. That is not what this country is all about.

"The unvarnished truth is that the tax code is a chain around the throat of the poor."

I have ample personal evidence of the regressive and punitive nature of America's tax code. My great-great-grandparents were slaves. My great-grandparents were sharecroppers who owned no land, no homes, and no businesses. They had no sellable assets other than their own "sweat equity." I can still recall my maternal great-grandfather, who was born in 1871—eight years after the Emancipation Proclamation was signed. He died at the age of 97, and the "estate" he left his family was his good name and his reputation.

My grandparents were farmers who lived off small parcels of land because, at the time, there were few other alternatives for providing food, shelter, and clothing for their families. When my maternal grandfather died at the age of 93, his estate was that parcel of land, a small house for my grandmother to live out her days, and his good name and reputation. My 102-year-old grandmother still lives in that house.

My father was the first in our family not to make his living off the land because, by the 1950s, a small dirt farm was not a viable way for a man to provide for his family and pursue the dream of owning more than "sweat equity." Instead, he worked three jobs at once—as chauffeur, barber, and janitor—to help send his two sons to college and accumulate some property. When my father died at age 56, his estate included his good name and his reputation, plus enough in assets to provide for my mother for the rest of her days.

It took three generations after slavery for my family to reach the point today where they can enjoy the progress made possible by hard work and strong character. Three generations is a long time to produce first-generation college graduates and, in my case, a restaurant business owner.

My journey is typical of most minority business owners and of many other family-owned businesses. It has been a long, hard, tough climb, one that was made far more difficult by the tax code. Adding insult to injury is the fact that many families now face the prospect that estate taxes will penalize them for their progress and hard work. In fact, estate taxes penalized my father for choosing to work three jobs.

Punishing Those Who Do the Right Thing. Indeed, the estate tax is a perfect example of how our tax code has become a barrier to opportunity. The original idea behind the estate tax may have been to redistribute income from the very wealthy, but today the people affected most negatively by the estate tax are not the super-rich. The wealthy can find accountants and lawyers to shelter their estates. In the end, the estate tax is not a tax on wealth, but a tax on first-generation business owners who have struggled mightily to gain a stake in our economy. That is plain wrong, and it is certainly counterproductive if we want to maintain a sound, healthy, and progressive economy.

The punitive effect of estate taxes is merely one small example of what is wrong with our tax code. Family businesses, the American Dream, and the free enterprise system are all threatened by the current tax system. Only 30 percent of family businesses or farms make it through the second generation. Only 13 percent make it through the third generation. As noted, it took my family three generations to arrive at the point where we feel enfranchised, and we now face the prospect of having our dreams taken away from us.

And what of the person who is working hard—perhaps at three jobs, like my father—to earn what he or she hopes will provide income to invest and save? To understand how heavy the tax burden is on savings and investment, consider this example:

A working mother finally puts together $100 of income and decides that, rather than spend it on clothing, food, or some other product or service, she will invest it to start a college fund for her young child. That is her dream—to send her child to college.

She chooses, perhaps using a financial planner, to purchase stock in a start-up company. She is fortunate, and the invest-

Chart 1.1

Investments Can Be Taxed Up to Four Times: Message to Taxpayer Is "Spend Now"

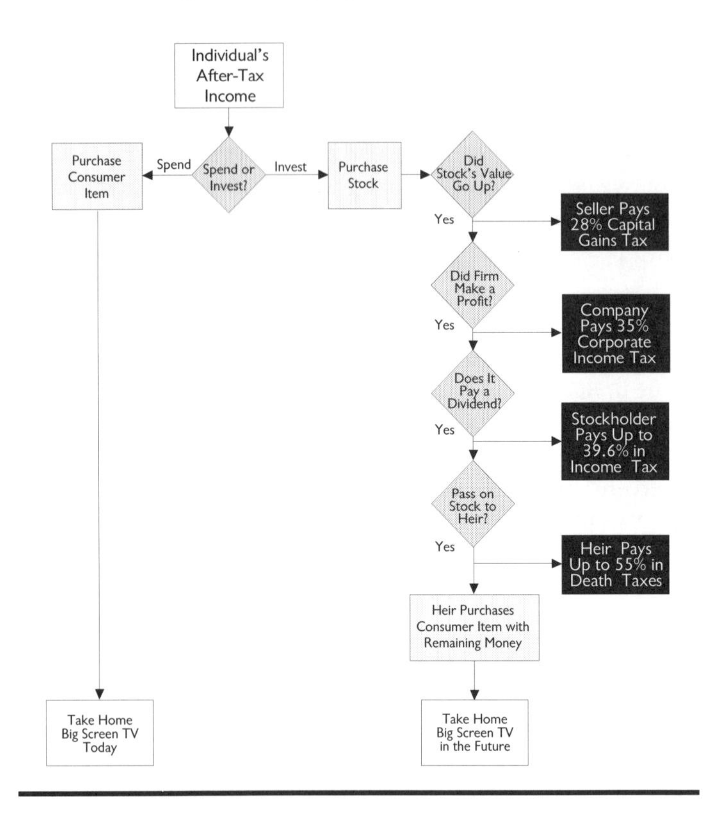

ment proves a good one. It yields a 10 percent rate of return, a $10 profit, which not only is good for her, but also indicates that the company is growing and providing jobs and producing goods the public needs.

Unfortunately, the tax code exacts a price for this success—a steep price. Under the current system, 35 percent of the $10 profit the company would award to the single mother is lost to corporate income tax, leaving her with $6.50. And this is merely the beginning. Depending on the investor's income, the personal income tax could take as much as 40 percent of the remaining $6.50—leaving only $3.90 of that $10 dividend.

Our working mother would not be in this tax bracket, but she would still be penalized for her successful investment. Adding insult to injury, she also faces applicable state and local income taxes on her investment.

Suppose this woman then decides to sell the stock. She will be hit with one of the world's highest capital gains taxes. Making a bad situation worse, she will be taxed on the nominal gains, meaning that taxes sometimes are paid on assets that have lost value in real terms.

In the United States, what we have is a tax code under which a fortunate investor—someone who earns money on his or her investments—might have to send more than 80 percent of those earnings to the government. And we are not even considering the taxes paid on the money used for the investment in the first place. This tax policy punishes savings and investment. We see our dreams deflated.

Consider that if our working mother had decided to spend her $100 savings on consumables, she would have incurred little or no federal tax liability. Our tax code encourages consumption rather than construction. Is it any wonder that the United States has one of the lowest savings rates in the world?

The bottom line is that this nation's tax code is punitive and impedes our prosperity by penalizing work, savings, and investment. We have to throw out what we have and start from scratch. So where do we go from here?

SIX PRINCIPLES OF TAX REFORM

The National Commission on Economic Growth and Tax Reform, on which I served in 1995 and 1996, proposed a structure for tax code reform. We developed Six Working Principles that I believe provide solid guideposts for policymakers to follow in order to create true, equitable economic opportunity for all Americans.

Six Principles of Tax Reform

- Any new tax code must encourage economic growth.
- Any new tax code must encourage fairness.
- Any new tax code must be simple.
- Any new tax code must be neutral.
- Any new tax code should promote visibility.
- Any new tax code should provide stability.

Source: National Commission on Economic Growth and Tax Reform, 1996.

Any new tax code must *encourage economic growth*. As the commission reported, "expanding opportunity, prosperity and social mobility form the foundation of a free and healthy society." In this regard, it should be kept in mind that our nation has experienced three periods of robust economic growth—the 1920s, the 1960s, and the 1980s. In each instance, growth came on the heels of reductions in marginal tax rates, and real tax revenues rose appreciably. On the other hand, high tax rates traditionally have produced a smaller economy, which in turn meant a smaller tax base and less income to tax. We cannot tax our way to prosperity.

Any new tax code must *encourage fairness*, because "democracy is based on the principle of equality before the law." Survey research conducted by the Gallup Organization shows that, as recently as 1961, about half of all Americans polled believed their federal income taxes were "about right." By 1982, 60 percent thought their income taxes were too high. By 1994, 66 percent were dissatisfied with their rate, and only a year later, according to a poll commissioned by *Reader's Digest*, 68 percent felt their tax payments were excessive.

That same poll commissioned by *Reader's Digest* found a remarkable consensus on the issue of tax fairness. Across the board, regardless of age, sex, race, or political persuasion, respondents agreed that 25 percent was the highest rate a family of four should have to pay. In order to bring Americans back to the point at which they consider the tax system fair, we must satisfy three goals: treat everyone equally; treat those least able to pay with compassion; and keep the tax rate low.

"Our code today punishes those who would save and promotes consumption. It promotes one way of life over another."

Any new tax code must *be simple*, because "life is too short and peace of mind too precious to waste your time and lose your temper trying to figure out your taxes." Any system that encourages the distribution of 8 billion pages of forms and instructions annually is far too complicated, as is any system that is managed by 62 million lines of computer code. All of this tells us that the current tax code is too expensive to administer, too difficult to enforce, and frustratingly impossible to understand. The long and short of it: keep things simple.

Any new tax code must *be neutral*; "the tax code should not pick winners or play favorites, but allow people to freely make decisions based on their needs and dreams." The example of the working mother demonstrates how the tax code can hamstring the freedom to make decisions, and thereby constrain or destroy dreams. Our code today punishes those who would save and promotes consumption. It promotes one way of life over another. Writer Joel Belz perhaps stated it best in the February 3, 1996, issue of *World*: "The power to tax is indeed the power to destroy, but by extension it is also the power to shape a society's values and ideals—and in doing so to establish which freedoms will be promoted and which will be restricted." A neutral tax code promotes freedom.

HOW THE FLAT TAX SATISFIES THE PRINCIPLES OF REFORM

Where does this lead us? Two major plans have been proposed to overhaul the U.S. tax code: the flat tax and the national retail sales tax. Either of these would improve on what we have by replacing a discriminatory tax structure with a single low rate. Either would eliminate the current code's bias against savings and investment. And with either one, the Internal Revenue Service, with all of its complicated forms and bewilderingly complex rules and regulations, would be downsized.

My personal preference is for the flat tax proposal. This approach satisfies the Six Working Principles outlined above.

- **It would encourage economic growth** by, among other things, eliminating the double, triple, and often quadruple taxation of income generated through savings and investment. This, in turn, would do away with the promotion of consumption over savings and investment.
- **Fairness would be promoted** through a single tax rate. A taxpayer earning 20 times more than his neighbor would pay 20 times more in taxes. It is that simple. There would be no special loopholes, no deductions, no reductions, and no exceptions.
- **There is nothing simpler than the flat tax.** Under a flat tax, our complicated, confusing, 600 or so tax forms could be replaced by two postcard-size forms—one for business and capital income, the other for individual income. This would reduce appreciably the 5.4 billion hours it takes Americans to

complete federal tax forms, and it would cut the $157 billion spent by the private sector to comply with income tax laws.

- **Neutrality would be established** under a flat tax proposal by taxing all income equally, thereby removing the system from the hands of policymakers and regulators. There would be no picking of winners or losers, so the tax code no longer could manipulate society's values and ideals.
- **Visibility would be encouraged** with the establishment of the percentage tax that every taxpayer would be required to pay. This percentage would be determined by the cost of government. Total revenues raised through taxation would provide our citizens with a number that establishes the cost of government. We finally would know what we are paying for government.
- **Due to its simplicity, the flat tax would not encourage tinkering and changing.** There would not be 17,000 pages of laws and regulations to adjust or "fine tune." There would not be pages upon pages of small print that beg rewriting. We would have a stable tax code that allowed Americans to plan for the future, knowing that it is difficult to add fine print to a postcard-size tax form.

When we have created a fair, simple, neutral, transparent, stable tax code that promotes economic progress for everybody in this great nation, we will have taken a giant step toward making the American Dream a reality for all. By taking this very necessary action, we will make the pursuit of happiness an attainable goal for many who, today, are effectively disenfranchised by our tax laws. The pursuit of happiness should be the function of one's aspirations, motivation, and determination. If we unleash the potential in people, they will pursue their aspirations, fueled by motivation and determination.

People want to be able to dream and to pursue their dreams. As Dr. Benjamin E. Mays, late President Emeritus of Morehouse College, said, "It isn't a calamity to die with dreams unfulfilled, but it is a calamity not to dream."

REALIZING THE AMERICAN DREAM

It has been my experience that when people begin to believe in their dreams, things happen. Borrowing from my own experience again, I can tell you that this is not merely "pie in the sky" thinking. I was raised in the segregated South, where schools for blacks were seldom of the same caliber as those for whites. I had a teacher who told me I was getting an inferior education.

Fortunately, I also had a teacher who encouraged me to make the most of my education by "working a little harder, and working a little longer." I finished high school second in my class and applied to and was accepted at Morehouse College. I was the first of my family to attend college, and I graduated.

From there, I worked for the Department of the Navy (civil service) and, while employed, decided to pursue a master's degree at Purdue University. Once again, someone told me that I would never make it. I did, and after four years with the Coca-Cola Company, I was hired by the Pillsbury Company. I worked hard and advanced to vice president of corporate systems and services.

I was pleased and proud of what I had accomplished, but my dream was to be president of something, somewhere. After consulting with people I trusted at Pillsbury, I decided to enter the company's Burger King division. I resigned my title, gave up a company car, let my stock options go, and started making hamburgers, sweeping floors, and cleaning bathrooms. This was the way to make my dream come true, and I pursued it. I completed a two-year training program in nine months and ended up as vice president of the Philadelphia region. Then, with the help of some good people, we turned around one of the worst performing regions and made it Burger King's best in growth, sales, and profits.

Pillsbury came to me when things were going well at Burger King and asked if I would like to be president of Godfather's Pizza, Inc., another division of the company. It was my dream come true, with a small problem. Godfather's was in serious financial trouble. Again, with the help of some good people and a great deal of hard work, we managed to get Godfather's focused and back on track.

A few months later, I partnered with another executive and we bought Godfather's from Pillsbury. I am living proof that if you want something bad enough—and are willing to work hard enough no matter the obstacles—you can make it happen.

I believe we must apply this same thinking and determination to changing the tax code. We must believe that it can be accomplished. We must overcome the naysayers. They will tell us it is an impossible task, just as the naysayers said the original 13 colonies could not obtain their liberty from the British. It is not impossible. They will tell us the forces arrayed against us are too powerful, too formidable. Indeed, they are powerful and formidable, but we must refuse to be intimidated. The tax code is punitive; it is hobbling the talents of many Americans, good people who deserve a chance to succeed. The tax code is wrong, and it must be changed.

Finally, the opposition will attempt to distract us with a laundry list of alternatives designed to interrupt our focus. We must stay on course, determined to do the job. If we do not, a bad situation can become immeasurably worse.

Consider that 50 years ago, Tax Freedom Day—the day on which Americans stop working for the government and start working for themselves—fell on March 25. In 1998, Tax Freedom Day fell on May 10. It has been projected that in 50 years, Tax Freedom Day will not arrive until sometime in early sum-

Chart 1.2

During the 1980s, People Who Started in the Lowest Income Quintile Were More Likely to End Up "Rich" Than to Have Stayed Poor

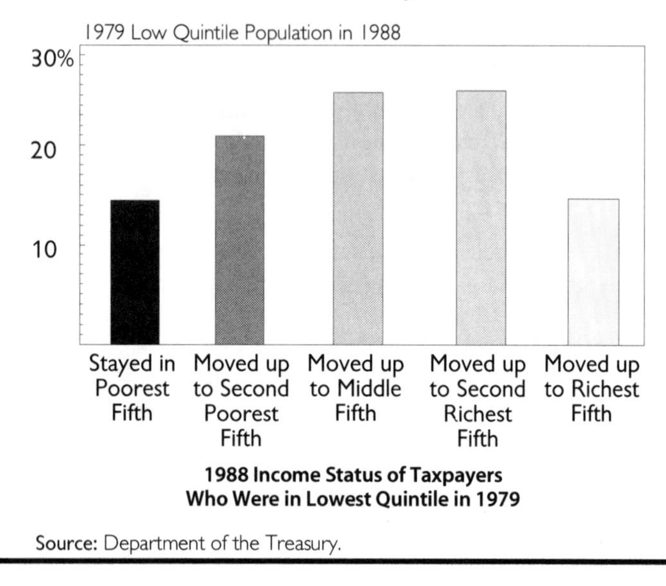

Source: Department of the Treasury.

mer. If that is the case, the individual freedoms, dreams, and aspirations of our grandchildren will have been smothered.

CONCLUSION

It is a grim possibility that the American system so many have sacrificed to build and maintain will not be able to survive. And it will have been subverted from within.

We cannot and must not allow that to happen. We can, must, and will create a fair, simple, neutral, transparent, stable tax code that promotes the economic growth of all Americans while ensuring that the true greatness of our country can be fulfilled.

Malcolm Wallop, founder and Chairman of the Frontiers of Freedom Institute, is a third-generation rancher from Big Horn, Wyoming. He was elected to the U.S. Senate in 1976 and served for 18 years, retiring in 1994. In addition to serving as ranking Republican member of the Energy and Natural Resources Committee, he served for ten years on the Intelligence Committee and four years on the Armed Services Committee. In 1981, Congress enacted legislation sponsored by Senator Wallop to cut inheritance and gift taxes—an effort hailed as one of the decade's major legislative achievements in tax reform. Mr. Wallop received his B.A. degree in literature from Yale University.

2

TODAY'S TAX CODE FOSTERS CORRUPTION

The Honorable Malcolm Wallop
Former U.S. Senator from Wyoming
Distinguished Fellow, The Heritage Foundation

"The power to tax involves the power to destroy." We repeat the wisdom of Justice John Marshall here because we say it almost by rote, and it tends to lose meaning. We need to hear it anew and couple it with Lord Acton's maxim that "Power tends to corrupt and absolute power corrupts absolutely."

Today, we see our government designed to protect the rights of citizens exercising the power to destroy through a complicated and ever-changing tax code. By corruption, I do not mean lying on a tax return or bribing a Member of Congress to alter the tax law. Those things may happen, but I am referring to how the power to tax, with its ever-present power to destroy, has created a profoundly corrupting ambience that engulfs even otherwise honest participants. It occurs at all levels—among those who write the tax laws, among those who enforce their collection, and among those who actually pay the taxes.

Ironically, even though America has the world's highest level of compliance, it is the tax code itself that breeds dishonesty and corruption. This does not mean that we have become a nation of tax cheats. Quite the contrary: We have become a nation of tax victims. We are besieged by complicated tax laws, confounded by unintelligible tax rules, manipulated by tax writers, and threatened by tax collectors. Corruption, whether intended or just absorbed through circumstances, is present at every level.

Tax writers in Washington, both elected officials and staff, have the power to create wealth or destroy it, provide favors or deny them, reduce competition or enhance it. Tax collectors have those powers, as well as the power of intimidation. Taxpayers are encouraged by the code to change their behavior, their marital status, their corporate structure, and even their civic standing to obtain benefits, not from their own creative or economic judgment, but from the tax preparers' view of how to qualify for beneficial treatment.

There are several truths that illustrate how the tax code degrades our national character:

- The more complicated the code, the more power the tax writers obtain over all taxpayers, both corporate and individual. If power corrupts—and it surely does—the dominion over taxpayers is absolutely corrupting.
- The more complicated the code, the more arbitrary the tax collector's exercise of power.
- The more unintelligible the rule and the more complicated the law, the more the taxpayer resorts to a sort of Darwinian compliance that is driven by survival through contortion and contrivance.

"Tax writers in Washington, both elected officials and staff, have the power to create wealth or destroy it, provide favors or deny them, reduce competition or enhance it."

THE POWER OF THE TAX WRITERS

Having served nearly 16 years on the Senate tax-writing committee, I learned a few things. I was never so naïve as to think my charm alone brought all those chief executive officers and lobbyists to my office, but I did believe that these people thought my views and strategies were important.

Today is different. For starters, I don't have nearly as many invitations to play golf as I once did. Did they seek to buy me, or did I sell myself for a golf game—or, for that matter, for a dinner or a speaking fee? Did interested parties want special access? Was there anything wrong, corrupt, or dishonest about it? While I believe my actions were always honest and based on principle, a Member of Congress with dishonorable tendencies can profit immensely.

> *TRUTH 1: Washington gains power by increasing the tax code's complexity.*

There are two institutional reasons why tax policy always seems to get worse. The first is that tax bills have to be revenue neutral, making it very difficult to provide across-the-board tax relief. The second is static scoring, which means that lawmakers are not allowed to include the beneficial effects that sound tax policy will have on job creation and economic growth. Combined, these factors cause tax policy to be a zero-sum game that pits one taxpayer against another and encourages gimmicks.

Revenue Neutrality. Revenue neutrality was then and remains today the source of more political logrolling than anything Congress has ever done. Relief is solely the product of someone else's grief. That is real power, and its exercise is corrupting even if the only currency is votes. The seductiveness of having solid citizens as dependents is never so clear as when they are seeking special changes in the tax code.

Even in years when we were not raising taxes, we tinkered with the code and made it more complex (over my objections). Not coincidentally, politicians benefit from this system. Only in 1986 was there the pretense of real reform, so in other years something else drove the activity. Take my word for it: Nobility was not the motive.

Targeted tax credits are special-interest feeding frenzies. Narrowly focused and politically visible, they generate both financial and political support for politicians. Even better, a Member can claim to be a "conservative tax cutter" even though these credits are the equivalent of spending programs. There are countless special-interest provisions in the tax code. I remember with disbelief, for example, the credits for buying wood-burning stoves during the Carter-era energy crisis. Now such stoves are largely outlawed in many towns because of their pollution effects, but we elected officials enjoyed the favorable press at the time.

Tuition tax credits are another wonder. Of course, tax preferences are responsible for the education of the children of the hard-pressed middle class, are they not? Yet statistics show that one of the reasons college tuition outpaces inflation derives specifically from higher education's skill at becoming a principal beneficiary of government favors. The parents run in place while increased tuition costs absorb their promised relief.

"Targeted tax credits are special-interest feeding frenzies."

This may not be a direct form of corruption, but it is an exercise of power to obtain political credit without identifying the cost. Its intent is to deceive the taxpayer. To that extent, it is a temptation to elected officials who publicly decry tax loopholes and added complication but apply the former and expand the latter without hesitation and without political blame.

Special-Interest Deductions. In *Money for Nothing*, Fred McChesney points out that campaign contributions and other expressions of interest arise as much from the threat to tax as from the promise not to. The threat of a tax is a second cousin to extortion rackets. In every instance when the Finance Com-

Chart 2.1

Both Lobbyists and Tax Regulations Have Tripled in the Last 30 Years

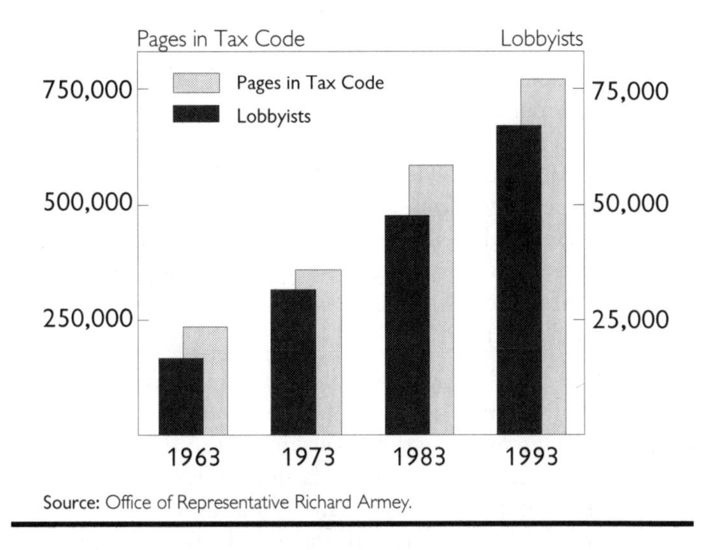

Source: Office of Representative Richard Armey.

mittee opened the Code (and there were 14 such occasions during my 16 years there), every American's interests were at stake. Thousands of tax lawyers, industry interests, personal interests, corporate interests, charitable interests, state tax interests, and even tax preparer's interests were involved, and they gathered to express them.

They lobbied congressional staff, elected officials, and Treasury bureaucrats. Why? Because these people could carve out exceptions, grant relief, design phase-outs or phase-ins, conceal treasures, and postpone or retroactively impose penalties. It was their role to provide access and to determine fates. Clearly, the more complicated the code became, the more opportunities arose to do mischief or grant favors. Those who wrote the laws commanded attention. The less clear the provisions, the greater the anxieties. The greater the anxieties, the larger the contributions. The larger the presence, the more muffled became the lesser voices.

For the most part, there is nothing dishonest about expressing an interest, but access is key to getting a hearing, and power and money produce results. For example, throughout my time in the Senate, American automobile manufacturers wanted the tax code to penalize foreign automobile manufacturers. Through tariffs or artful definitions of such terms as "gas-guzzler," politicians often found the way to do it. Consumers were rarely heard, even though their costs were increased. In the early 1980s, there were not many foreign car dealers, and practically none integrated with domestic makers. Their voices were muffled and rarely heard.

Complicated tax law provides full employment for special interests. By the time I left the Senate in 1994, there still were regulations implementing the provisions of the 1986 Tax Simplification Act that remained to be issued. However, the struggle over its ultimate contents began right after the 1984 elections as talk of tax reform emerged as the prime agenda of both parties. The political support was queasy, but the interest was intense. The entire Senate Finance Committee met in "retreat" in West Virginia with Secretary of the Treasury James Baker to resurrect reform. There emerged a promising simplification and reform proposal with bipartisan support. Immediately, the lobbying of outside interests rose to the crescendo described so aptly in Jeff Birnbaum's book, *Showdown at Gucci Gulch*.

The charities, for example, said they could not exist without charitable deductions. The president of Yale wrote to me and said that, without that provision, "Yale would cease to exist as the great private institution you have known it to be." I responded by noting that, to my great surprise, he had just informed me that Yale was not in fact a private institution after all, but a dependent of the government whose taxpayers had to support it by increasing their tax payments to cover the deductions of others.

New York State appealed to Senator Daniel Patrick Moynihan to restore the preference for state income taxes, or else there would be an out-migration to states with no such tax. Turn the coin over and it reads that all the rest of us must contribute to the excesses of those high-tax states by allowing their state taxes to be written off their federal obligation. It increases either the deficit or our taxes to cover it.

H&R Block and the accounting profession generally let it be known how many would become unemployed if we got carried away with simplification. Their lobbying was generous, as was that of every other interest in the nation. Was any of it blatantly corrupt? Probably not, but the point is that by the time the committee was finished, any arguable claim to simplification had been obliterated by a series of amendments. And worse was to come on the floor, and worse yet out of conference.

Providing personal tax relief to Americans meant that corporate obligations had to be increased enormously. A real estate industry whose benefits had been too generous now found itself on its back because Senator Bob Packwood led the charge against it. He was expressing a visceral dislike of some of its players and all of its actions. Senator Lloyd Bentsen and I warned of the consequences of having overcorrected by forecasting the collapse of the savings and loan industry.

We also vainly fought attempts to attack the always unpopular oil industry, but that political currency was stronger than ever. Who, for example, would argue that personal tax relief should be reduced to save the oil industry? Revenge is not corruption, but neither is it logical. The temptation to exercise it becomes a clear demonstration of what happens when you get on the wrong side of the tax writers. Is it any wonder, then, that contributions flow in to both parties from all sides?

There is yet one other area in which a form of corruption exists. It is in the staff preparation of the work product, after mark-up, or floor action, or conference. Congressional staffers and IRS officials have a vested, personal interest in a complex tax code. After all, the more complicated the system, the greater the demand for their services after they depart the public sector. Who else would know how to interpret convoluted tax laws?

To illustrate this phenomenon, one has to go no further than the pension plan provisions of the 1986 Tax Reform Act. Certain conference committee staffers added language prohibiting "discrimination" in pension plan structures. A bleary-eyed, unsuspecting Congress passed the measure without notice. To this day, no one knows what the anti-discrimination provisions mean, nor does anyone—taxpayers, IRS agents, or scholars—have the slightest idea how to apply them. One group, however, has come out ahead. These former staffers are employed, largely at far greater salaries, promising to make sense of the confusion they created.

There are numerous other examples of Members finding provisions for which they had never voted mysteriously appearing in the final product. Senator Cliff Hansen, my predecessor on the Senate Finance Committee, told me how a $500,000 cap on the exemption for agricultural estate taxes came to be. In a 1978 tax bill, Senator Hansen asked Senator Abe Ribicoff to join him in providing relief from estate taxes to farmers and ranchers who stayed on their land for ten years after the death of the parent. Senator Ribicoff liked the idea and said he would join if Hansen would expand it to include small business proprietors as well. It passed unanimously in the committee and handsomely in the Senate.

When they got to conference, however, the two Senators were surprised to see that the amount that could be passed on to the children without being double-taxed had been capped at $1 million. They asked Chairman Russell Long where the cap had come from, and he said he didn't know. But, upon inquiring, Long discovered that his staff director had inserted it on his own because *he* didn't think it was appropriate uncapped. The House had no similar provision, so the compromise cut the amount in half. Thanks to the bias of one senior staffer, a good idea was twisted and the tax law became more complicated.

THE POWER OF TAX COLLECTORS

It has to be recognized that a complicated code strengthens the hand of tax collectors. It licenses arbitrary enforcement and subjective application. *Money* magazine conducts an annual test of professional tax preparers, and none of them can calculate the taxes owed by a hypothetical family correctly. No two even manage to come up with the same answer.

> *TRUTH 2: Complexity allows tax collectors to apply their power arbitrarily.*

The IRS, meanwhile, does an even worse job, making millions upon millions of mistakes every year. None of this gives comfort to the taxpayer confronted with an IRS audit or challenge. To whom can he argue for relief? And should he fail to gain that relief, the agency's bottomless resources for litigation often mean that a citizen who knows in his heart that he has not cheated is forced, by the threat of added penalties and interest, to submit. The cost to prove innocence is out of all proportion to the cost of capitulation. This enormous power has increased as Congress has complicated the code. Congress is complicit in what can be described only as a savage assault on the free status of the citizenry.

Chart 2.2

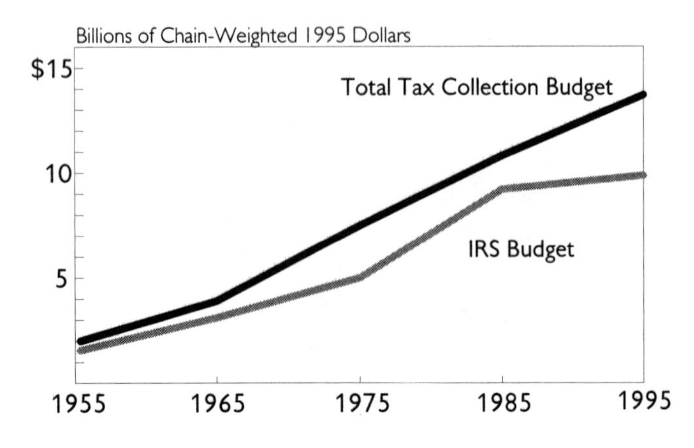

Source: Heritage calculations, based on Tax Foundation data.

Back in 1982 and 1984, during the reconciliation process when the Budget Committee assigned revenue targets to each committee, we on the Finance Committee discovered two things:

1. To reach our assigned goals, we could not reduce any appropriations for Treasury or for the IRS, as that was solely within the dominion of the Appropriations Committee.
2. We had only two means by which to achieve our targets: raise taxes yet again or *hire more IRS agents*.

Hiring more agents in those days was thought to be a revenue raiser, so we began adding 30,000 new guns. Can anyone be surprised that, if agents are scored as revenue raisers, the bosses set out to prove that truth? This licensed arrogance. It licensed the view that citizens were uniformly corrupt and that the agent's job was to ferret us out and bring us to heel. An agency never known to be cordial became in many respects utterly lawless. The innumerable stories of abuses in the congressional hearings of 1997 sobered even the President, but they only touched the outer limits.

IRS Arrogance. In one instance recounted by James Bovard in the *American Spectator*, the family of Clayton and Darlene Powell became the target of outrageous IRS abuse caused by the agency's own clerical errors. The IRS threatened the Powells with fines. It threatened to seize their property. Forced to pay, the Powells sued for a refund. The court of appeals ruled that the Powells were entirely innocent.

Undaunted, and in imperial fashion, IRS Commissioner Margaret Richardson announced that the IRS would not be bound by the appeals court ruling. In her view, the court had misinterpreted the law! The agency declared itself to be in *non-acquiescence*. Henceforth, it would be bound only by individual court rulings in individual cases, leaving the rest of the citizenry subject to its continued whimsy.

So much, indeed, for the concept that we are a nation of laws. This is profoundly corrupting, and stems directly from a code now so complicated that neither the courts nor the agency can interpret it consistently.

IRS Quotas. The pressure on the agency to perform leads to other instances of corruption. Managers have been accused of cooking statistics to receive merit pay. Agents have been assigned numerical targets for collection. Until recently, there has even been an unlimited presumption in tax law that the agency is always right and that the taxpayer must prove it wrong.

The reforms of last year slightly improved this situation, but the overall impact will be modest—especially if, as it is wont to do, the agency targets those taxpayers least able to defend themselves.

Taxing Behavior. More proof of the corruption caused by a complicated code is that Commissioner Margaret Richardson felt entitled to expand an audit concept called the Taxpayer Compliance Measurement Program, or TCMP. Henceforth, according to Richardson, it would be appropriate to audit the taxpayer's lifestyle in addition to his tax return. The economic behavior of taxpayers, such as the cars they drive, the restaurants they frequent, the resorts they visit, and even the clothes they wear, was deemed to demonstrate ability to pay.

The agency, as usual, had given no thought to the cost to the individual taxpayer of complying with such an audit, or to the enormous indignity of having to supply it, or to the fear of invasion of privacy engendered by agents' ever more innovative applications. A clearer, simpler law could never have licensed such behavior.

HOW TAXPAYERS COMPLY

Complicated law, unintelligible rules, and unequal application drive taxpayers to behave in entirely unnatural ways. A former governor who is now President overvalued his used underwear as charitable gifts. Some couples who otherwise would marry choose to live together, at least in part to avoid the marriage penalty on their combined incomes. Phase-outs—those class-baiting devices of Congress that take away tax preferences above certain income levels—force people to understate, restate, or just stop adding to their income in order to qualify.

If anyone thinks that tax policies don't drive behavior, they should look at the famous tables developed by W. Kurt Hauser, Vice Chairman of the Hoover Institution, called the "19.5% Charts." Despite federal income tax rates that ranged from 91 percent to 28 percent over three decades, federal revenues have hovered around 19.5 percent of GNP. One can draw a couple of behavioral conclusions. When tax rates are too high, taxpayers either stop working or find loopholes. Shelters in the tax code provided hidden relief to some, and changes in the investment or earnings behavior of taxpayers provided the rest. Yet the country suffers because, without exception, the *periods of higher tax rates produce slower growth.*

In spite of this evidence, the Joint Tax Committee, the Treasury, and the Congressional Budget Office insist on static revenue scoring. Their theory is that if a tax at 10 percent produces $1,500, then one at 20 percent will produce $3,000. It is government's sheep theory. If citizens do one thing, then, like sheep, they will always do the same thing no matter what government does. Endless evidence points to rational behavior on the part of taxpayers; thus, one can only conclude that the only sheep whose behavior is predictable are the government estimators.

> *TRUTH 3: Complexity causes inventive compliance by taxpayers.*

To illustrate the point, President George Bush's infamous tax increase of 1990, which was driven by class-warfare politics, failed at every turn. It failed to generate the revenues forecast, and it even failed to produce as much revenue as before the increase. Furthermore, revenues from those earning more than $200,000 (the people whose taxes were raised) fell by more than 6 percent, while those earning less saw their tax payments increase by more than 1 percent. Tax writers provided some favors, but more important, "rich" taxpayers changed behavior to protect their earnings.

While taxpayers should be free to defend themselves, these tax complications impose a hidden cost because of contorted uneconomic behavior. This in turn requires intrusive enforcement techniques, which cost both resources to apply and confidence in equity after they are applied.

Another corrupting influence from added complications is that each targeted tax credit—whether for child care, education, minority or handicapped hiring, energy efficiency, or anything else—does two things. First, it sets up competition among the various potential beneficiaries and powerful special interests; and second, it enhances the whole sense of entitlement that is abroad in the land. Citizens fight each other trying to get their share of the pot and then, having qualified for the pot, seek to keep others out. Thus, once added, loopholes are almost impossible to remove.

One of the consequences of high tax rates, especially punitive death taxes, has been for some U.S. citizens to renounce their citizenship and move their assets offshore. This has enraged the tax collectors, Treasury officials, and some in Congress. Their response has been to seek to levy a wealth tax on these people. Notwithstanding the fact that those who sought to move had paid all their taxes through the years, the IRS feels that *these unpatriotic folk have to be punished.*

Back in the late 1970s, when the Soviet Union sought to impose such taxes on emigrating Jews, we called it a human rights violation. But those were communists, and we are Americans. Whether one likes the move or not, the behavior is driven not by lost patriotism, but by pure economics and the desire to protect family assets from yet another layer of taxation. The country would prosper far more by lowering the tax burden and harvesting the future productivity of these people.

CONCLUSION

The basic behavior of all three segments of our tax system—tax writers, tax collectors, and taxpayers—is driven less by fairness and logic than by power and privilege.

For the tax writers, it may be possible to rationalize providing targeted relief for a politically powerful constituency, financed by higher taxes on some other group; but a sale is a sale, whether it is for votes or for contributions.

For the tax collectors and enforcers, the idea of a lawless citizenry bent on deceit soon changes the attitude at the IRS from the mere collection of taxes to establishing enforcement quotas, invading privacy, bullying the less powerful, and rejecting court decisions. It also raises, out of taxpayers' sheer frustration and fear, physical threats to and assaults on agents themselves.

For the taxpayer faced with 17,000 pages of code and regulations, complexities beyond comprehension, and favors for some over others, corruption arises from the survival techniques needed to save money. Despair over complication drives some to fill out a form any way they can and hope it survives scrutiny. To dodge is considered fair even if it means, for example, living in sin instead of marriage.

Are these various players corrupt in the traditional sense of using their power for illegal or unjust gain? The answer, of course, is that some are, some always have been, and some are waiting for their chance. However, far more to the point is the fact that all elements of the tax code have corrupted our values.

Indeed, the current tax code corrupts every level of life and degrades our national character. Its complexities are a source of power. Clearly, the public would benefit from a stable tax regime, but 12,000 changes in 18 years show that tax writers prefer constant change.

Republicans and Democrats alike visit the tax code annually, for where else can they garner such attention surrounding their slightest moves? Until we have a President and a Congress clearly committed to purging the entire mess, these bizarre forms of corruption will compound exponentially. The temptations of the most honest will fall prey to ever-expanding opportunities to curry favor, votes, or even wealth.

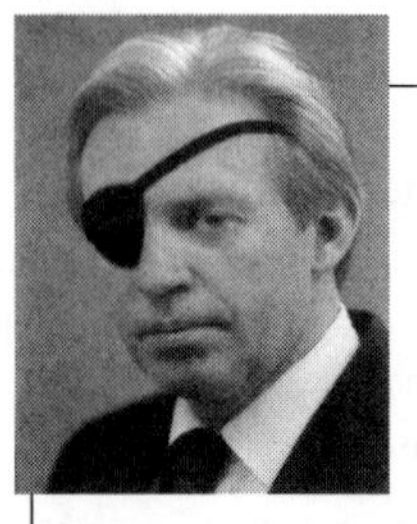

Dr. Richard Rahn, president of Novecon Ltd., served as Executive Director of the American Council for Capital Formation from 1976 to 1980 and as Vice President and Chief Economist of the U.S. Chamber of Commerce from 1980 to 1991. He also has served as National Executive Director of the Ripon Society. Dr. Rahn, a senior fellow of the Discovery Institute and member of the Mont Pelerin Society, was appointed by President Reagan to the Quadrennial Social Security Advisory Council in 1982. He has published articles in such national publications as *The Wall Street Journal* and *The New York Times*, and has testified before the U.S. Congress on more than 75 occasions. He received his Ph.D. in business economics from Columbia University.

3

THE IRS CHOICE: TAX REFORM OR SELF-DESTRUCTION

Richard W. Rahn, Ph.D.
Senior Fellow, Discovery Institute

The Internal Revenue Service (IRS) as it exists today is incompatible with a free society. It is intrusive and, by its very nature, contrary to the fundamental rights of citizens. Congressional and press investigations over the past half-century have detailed abuse after abuse of the people by the IRS. Yet, despite many attempts to rein in the agency through various taxpayer protection acts, the abuses continue, and they will continue as long as the present tax code and IRS remain.

The IRS cannot collect the revenue demanded by Congress without behaving in a manner inconsistent with personal freedom. To tax not only income, but also savings, investments, and assets, the government must know intimate details of each individual's financial situation. For the IRS to be all-knowing, by definition, the fundamental rights of privacy and fairness must be violated.

Thus, as many tax reformers and intelligent, honest politicians understand, having both an IRS and a free society is an oxymoron. Periodic reforms of the IRS have been attempted, but these efforts have been unsuccessful because of the voracious need of many politicians to confiscate some people's wealth in order to distribute it to their more favored constituents.

Fortunately for the beleaguered taxpayer, a technological revolution is coming. This chapter will explain why the current tax code and the IRS will not be able to survive in this new technological age any more than communism could survive the revolution in information technology. Just as the politicians did not tear down the Berlin Wall (the people did), politicians are unlikely to dissolve the IRS. But the people can, and they will through the digital revolution.

THE NEED FOR FUNDAMENTAL REFORM

The need for fundamental tax reform is now obvious to all but a few politicians, tax lawyers, and accountants who have a vested interest in the code's complexity and selective enforcement. Economists are concerned with improving its efficiency, and most would shift the burden away from taxing labor and capital (what people put into the economy) toward taxing consumption (what people take out of the economy).

There is a general acknowledgment that the complexity of the U.S. tax system has reached a level that is unmanageable not only for the average citizen, but even for the tax professional. Every April, a story appears in one or more of the business and financial publications that demonstrates that tax professionals are incapable of calculating the correct amount of tax for a hypothetical middle-income taxpayer.

"Just as the politicians did not tear down the Berlin Wall (the people did), politicians are unlikely to dissolve the IRS. But the people can, and they will through the digital revolution."

Typically, for these studies, income and spending details of the hypothetical taxpayer are provided to a number of the leading tax preparation firms and several IRS offices, and the tax professionals are asked to calculate the tax owed. As would be expected, each tax professional and each IRS office comes up with a different answer. All of this would be amusing if it were not for the fact that Mr. or Ms. Taxpayer could go to jail for a wrong answer, even if the wrong answer is provided by their accountant.

This is exactly what happened to New York hotelier Leona Helmsley. Mrs. Helmsley was very rich and was reputed to be "the queen of mean." An alleged comment that "only the little people pay taxes" made her a prime target for the IRS. According to a report in *The Wall Street Journal* in 1992, the Helmsleys paid $53.7 million in federal taxes on their adjusted gross income of $103.6 million. The IRS was not satisfied, and claimed that the Helmsleys had underreported their income by $2.6 million to evade $1.7 million in taxes.

Leona Helmsley was prosecuted for tax evasion, lost her case, and went to prison. She may or may not have been trying to cheat the IRS, but the trial circumstances made it apparent that she was targeted. Her case was a victory for selective law enforcement, a point reinforced when President Bill Clinton and his wife were found to have underpaid their taxes and made to pay only the amount they owed plus interest. Mrs. Helmsley's sentence of four years in the penitentiary is excessive compared with that given to Sophia Loren, who was restricted to a friend's home for 30 days for her offense of the same scale.

Fortunately, the American people have elected a few representatives to Congress who are determined to get rid of much of the complexity in the code. House Majority Leader Richard Armey (R–TX), a former professor of economics, has developed a flat tax proposal, and House Ways and Means Committee Chairman Bill Archer (R–TX) has developed a national sales tax alternative. Both approaches would be a vast improvement over the current tax code.

Chart 3.1

Kennedy Tax Cuts Boosted Tax Revenue

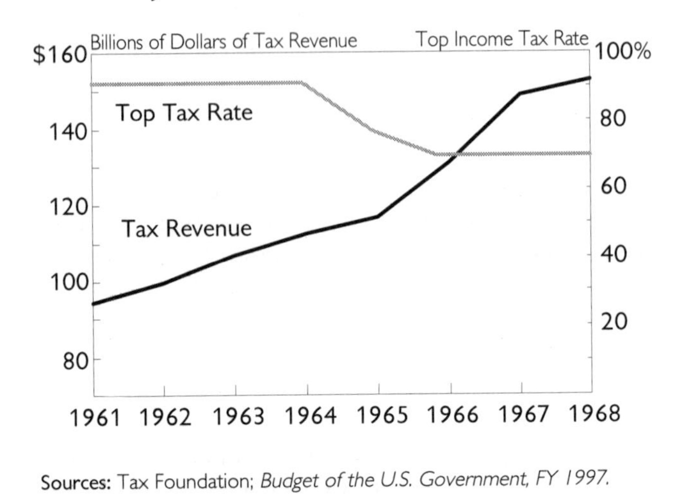

Sources: Tax Foundation; *Budget of the U.S. Government, FY 1997.*

Tax Rates and Tax Revenues Are Not Equal

A key ingredient in the success of any new tax system will be its rates—especially the marginal rate (the rate a taxpayer pays on the last dollar of income, or the highest rate any taxpayer pays). The most successful tax systems have low marginal rates. If the rate is low enough, most people will pay it without much complaint, and few will take steps to avoid it. History shows tax cuts have boosted revenue (see Charts 3.1 and 3.2).

On the other hand, high tax rate systems give huge rewards for tax evasion or avoidance. If the tax rate is 90 percent, then for every $100 you can avoid reporting, you get to keep an extra $90—a big incentive. If the tax rate is only 10 percent, then for every $100 you avoid reporting, you keep only $10—which, presumably, is not worth the risk of incurring a fine or jail sentence. High tax rates cause people to find legal or illegal ways

Chart 3.2

Tax Revenues Nearly Doubled During the 1980s Thanks to Reagan Tax Cuts

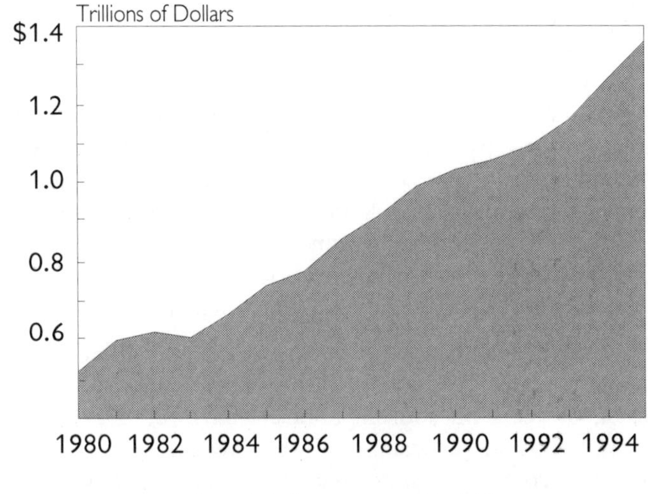

Source: *Budget of the U.S. Government, FY 1997.*

to avoid the tax, and they can always choose leisure (a non-taxed activity) over work (a taxed activity).

In recent years, economists have studied the rate at which different types of taxes maximize tax revenue. The longer the time period, the lower the rate needs to be to maximize revenue, because people will adjust their behaviors over time to minimize the tax. For example, a tax rate of 100 percent on income over the long run will produce no revenue, because no one will continue to work (or, at least, continue to report their work and income).

Likewise, a customs tax or sales tax needs to be sufficiently low to keep people from smuggling the product or refusing to purchase it. Recalling American history, the British tried to tax tea at too high a rate in 1773, and it ended up on the bottom of the Boston harbor rather than on the tables of the colonists.

The relationship between tax rates and tax revenues is commonly referred to as the Laffer Curve, after Professor Arthur B. Laffer. The Laffer Curve demonstrates that there are two tax rates that produce the same amount of revenue—a high rate (negative) and a low rate (positive). Rates in the negative range (high rates) will increase revenue when they are reduced, and rates in the positive range (low rates) will increase revenue when they are increased. For instance, a very high tax rate on labor will discourage people from working (at least in terms of reporting income to the government). If the tax rate is reduced, people will take jobs and/or report more income, and the tax revenue collected by the government will increase.

As Professor Laffer and others have noted, the difference between tax revenues and tax rates has been understood for at least 4,000 years, but foolish politicians have yet to learn that lesson. Politicians (as well as some tax lawyers, accountants, and even economists) have a hard time understanding that tax rates and tax revenues are not the same thing. At various times and in various places, politicians have managed to destroy many legitimate industries and create criminal ones by overtaxing the legitimate ones.

The Totalitarian Tactics of the IRS

In January 1997, Ann Reilly Dowd of *Money* magazine wrote the following:

> Dear Internal Revenue Service:
>
> Our two-month audit of your operations has determined that you are guilty of sloppy, discourteous and sometimes devious behavior. Your practices are so unacceptable, in fact, that if you were a US taxpayer, your pay could be garnished or

your property seized. But you're no small-fry US taxpayer; you're the all-powerful IRS. So when you mess up, you draw little more than anguished cries from law-abiding citizens and lawmakers alike. Meanwhile, taxpayers are being punished by your agency's unrepentant abuse of decent, hard-working individuals.

Later that year, the Senate held highly publicized hearings on such IRS abuses. These hearings, coupled with good investigative reporting, confirmed the worst fears of Americans about the Internal Revenue Service. Evidence was presented that the IRS:

- **Abused** taxpayers whom agents perceived were in a poor position to fight back;
- **Engaged** in practices designed to threaten and intimidate innocent taxpayers;
- **Has** an appallingly high error rate and consistently bills taxpayers for taxes they do not owe;
- **Used** a quota system for collections (which is illegal under the 1988 Taxpayer Bill of Rights) even though, in many cases, taxpayers did not owe what the IRS demanded;
- **Drove** some taxpayers to suicide;
- **Refused** to pay court-ordered judgments to taxpayers and continued litigating—at taxpayer expense—until some taxpayers were driven into bankruptcy or died;
- **Rarely disciplined or fired** poor employees, even when they violated the law;
- **Violated** the principle of confidentiality when agents looked at the returns of friends, relatives, and enemies;

- **Kept** poor records and destroyed some taxpayers' records deliberately; and
- **Made** audits of the IRS records impossible for at least the past four years.

These were not mere allegations. The Internal Revenue Service eventually acknowledged these facts and apologized to the American people after the hearings.

Not only has the IRS become far more intrusive, but the government has become far more vindictive toward citizens caught in its snares. In most countries, the sanction for a tax violation is a reasonable fine. Imprisonment for tax violations is rare, and when imposed, sentences are usually short. In the United States, however, the situation is far less benign. A barbaric punishment, for example, was given to a woman named Trula Walker in Kansas City in 1988. Convicted for tax evasion, she was sentenced to 30 years in jail—in stark contrast to the number of people convicted of murder in Washington, D.C., who are out of jail within a few years.

America is supposed to be the home of the free, yet it shares with Sweden and the former Soviet Union the global record for the most onerous and brutal penalties for tax evasion. Modern non-communist Russia has only monetary penalties for tax evasion in all but the most extreme cases. Ironically, in the United States, as author Charles Adams wrote in *For Good and Evil: The Impact of Taxes on the Course of Civilization*,

> our tax bureaucracy is, indeed, like a miniature Soviet state with the power to intimidate just about everyone, and this is because of the synthetic crimes Congress has manufactured to make these tax police, especially the IRS criminal division, masters of the art of intimidation.

The IRS has adopted a number of the old habits of totalitarian regimes, one of which is paying informers. Those who give the

Chart 3.3

A Fleet of Government Tax Collectors

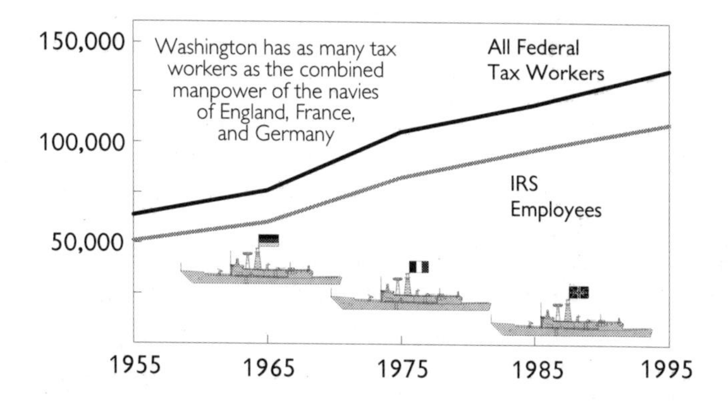

Sources: Tax Foundation; International Institue for Strategic Studies, *The Military Balance.*

IRS information that leads to a tax recovery can get as much as 10 percent of the first $75,000 recovered, 5 percent of the next $25,000, and 1 percent of the additional amount recovered. Such activity may be cost-effective for the IRS, but it engenders mistrust and deceit, rather than civil society—which should be the object of good governance.

The good news is that the horror, corruption, and abuse that people have been suffering at the hands of tax collectors under both totalitarian and democratic governments is not a necessary condition, nor is it one that should be as prevalent in the future digital age.

THE DIGITAL REVOLUTION

"[I]n this world nothing can be said to be certain, except death and taxes," Benjamin Franklin said. But what governments cannot see, they cannot tax; and, as a result of the digital revolution, the government will see only financial capital (assets and income) that is revealed voluntarily. The revolution taking place in electronic money means that banks and other organizations will be able to create their own money for transactional or investment purposes and literally move this money around the globe at the speed of light.

This is bad news for the IRS but good news for freedom. Money as government-created legal tender will become less and less relevant, and the existing distinctions between money, goods, services, and assets will disappear as they become even more interchangeable. When the definition of money itself becomes blurred, then that which can be transformed instantaneously into something else—and moved anywhere in the world with no paper or electronic trail—will become nearly impossible to tax. For example, by using public key cryptography, one can have electronic bank notes certified without the issuer knowing to whom they were issued. Smart cards used as an electronic purse can have the same anonymity as paper cash.

> *"Government officials have two choices: redesign the tax system to reflect technological reality or try to create a system in which every investment and expenditure by every person is known."*

The government cannot stop this revolution because it is global, and too many people around the world now have the knowledge. Censorship and regulation will not work, because those who are developing the means of evasion will always be far ahead of those who are trying to restrict them. Increasingly, clever people go to work for computer software and hardware companies rather than government agencies, because that is where the action and the opportunities for advancement are.

Indeed, most totalitarian governments (with the exception of China, North Korea, Cuba, and a few others) have largely given up trying to control the flow of information completely, because technology has made it a fruitless task.

Government officials have two choices: redesign the tax system to reflect technological reality or try to create a system in which every investment and expenditure by every person is known. In the new world of digital freedom, there is no middle ground, because if any privacy is granted, then all sensitive information can be hidden in that digital "drawer." A government which attempts to be all-knowing is doomed to failure, both practically and politically.

What Can Be Taxed in the Digital Age. If taxpayers can easily avoid reporting particular types of income or transactions and face virtually no danger of being caught because of technological innovations, then the tax becomes, quite literally, voluntary. A tax is voluntary when it is paid only by conscientious citizens who abide by the tax laws out of a sense of duty and honor rather than out of fear of civil or criminal penalties. Yet a genuinely voluntary tax is not a formula for responsibility and fairness, because a disproportionate share of the burden will be borne by those who choose not to evade the tax.

Assuming politicians want to keep the tax code from self-destructing, this has major implications for how a new tax code should be designed. It will be effectively impossible, for instance, for the tax base (what is taxed) of the future to include financial capital (productive savings). Why? Because financial capital can become invisible too easily. Encryption technology will allow taxpayers to protect capital transactions—including interest, dividends, and capital gains—from the government. As a result, the cost of enforcing the taxation of financial capital probably will exceed revenues collected. Furthermore, such enforcement certainly will exact a price in terms of lost efficiency and lost privacy rights.

Instead, the future tax base will have to rely on real and tangible property, payments by institutions to individuals and other institutions, and payments for tangible goods. Why? Taxes tied to real property or tangible personal property, or to the sale of goods and services to the public, are much more difficult to evade. Taxes tied to the employer–employee relationship (with the exception of domestic workers under the "nanny tax") are enforceable because of the stability, length, and visibility of the relationship. Taxes tied to the operation of businesses dealing with the public or with many business customers are enforced more easily because of the necessarily public and open nature of such businesses.

The Good News. Fortunately, the tax code that is feasible in the digital age is the one we should have anyway. More specifically, the current tax code over-taxes income that is saved and invested, and this will not be possible in the future. And as the tax burden on capital declines, higher rates of economic growth and higher real incomes for most people are likely to occur.

> *"Taxing capital is equivalent to destroying the 'seed corn' of the economy."*

Taxing capital is equivalent to destroying the "seed corn" of the economy. In the modern economy, a business must "save" enough, above what it pays out in wages, expenses, and dividends to stockholders, to buy new equipment and pay for research and development if it is to prosper in the future. When the government confiscates business profits, the business has less to invest in new equipment and research and development.

This translates directly into lower productivity growth, which in turn means lower real economic growth and slower growth in personal income. When the government taxes an individual's interest receipts, dividends, and capital gains, it both discourages that individual from saving and reduces the amount of money that individual could invest in productive activities.

Even though good economists have long known that imposing heavy taxes on capital—that is, corporate profits, capital gains, interest, and dividends—is counterproductive, the United States and many other countries continue to do so. The reason for such short-sighted tax policy is class-warfare politics. Some rich people earn a great deal of income from capital gains, interest, and dividends.

Such reasoning ignores the fact that the income that produces capital gains, interest, and dividends already has been taxed at least once, if not more. Moreover, lower-income people who are most dependent on added growth to improve their living standards would be the greatest beneficiaries of lower taxes on capital. Lowering the taxes on capital also frees money for other purposes. This extra money, for example, can be spent to expand a business and hire more employees.

Taxation of capital also destroys upward mobility, since an artificial "capital shortage" denies potential entrepreneurs the opportunity to better themselves. It is hypocritical for politicians, many of whom have never had a private-sector job, to propose and enact higher taxes on capital gains—which is a tax on *becoming* wealthy, as opposed to *being* wealthy.

Capital investment creates jobs. How many truck drivers would there be if there were no trucks to drive because there were no funds to buy them? Countries that have little capital also have high unemployment rates and low incomes.

The U.S. taxation of capital is relatively high compared with taxation of consumption; hence, the United States imports (borrows) capital from countries that tax consumption more heavily and capital less heavily. This accounts for the U.S. trade deficit. Those who wish to invest in the United States because of its economic and political stability and relatively high rate of return on capital need dollars to invest. They obtain dollars by selling goods or a service to Americans. If foreigners did not want dollars, America would not have a trade deficit.

If the United States had lower taxes on capital, Americans would save more and borrow less from foreigners. This in turn would lower the U.S. trade deficit and increase the rate of domestic investment, which would lead to higher real incomes.

TAX FREEDOM IN THE DIGITAL AGE

America's tax system used to be a non-intrusive system. Banks were not spies for the IRS and did not report cash withdrawals or interest income. The only reports the IRS received about a taxpayer were wage withholding statements (a practice which began in the early 1940s). Stock and real estate transactions, dividends, and other income were not reported to the IRS. Individuals reported these sources of income at the end of the year.

For the most part, this honor system—a system compatible with a free society—worked. The taxpayer was considered innocent until proven guilty. Under the current system, however, the government does not have to prove a taxpayer's guilt; the accused must prove his innocence. (This egregious practice, which is contrary to our Constitution, was modified slightly by Congress in 1998.)

The movement away from the honor system came about in part because of the advent of new technologies (especially computers) that enabled the government to keep detailed records of people's behavior. Ironically, these same technologies now are giving individuals the ability to regain a good deal of the financial privacy they once enjoyed.

Many of those who seek to regulate digital money, "smart cards," the Internet, and other developments in the digital age claim that if they do not regulate them, tax avoidance and tax evasion will occur. As usual, those with totalitarian mind-sets miss the point. They are correct in asserting that tax evasion and tax avoidance will increase—unless the tax laws are changed to reflect the digital reality. They are wrong, however, in asserting that more regulation will succeed in coaxing much more tax revenue from unwilling payers.

Again, the fact is that the digital revolution is going to make some tax evasion very easy, and increasing numbers of people will take advantage of that fact. If they can sit at home and, with a few key strokes on their computers, avoid paying tax, then many will choose to avoid paying taxes. An example drawn from a chapter in a 1997 book, *The Future of Money in the Information Age*, will help to illustrate how the digital revolution will change financial transactions.

Assume you are a lawyer in New York doing work for a client in a jurisdiction without an income tax. You send the work to your client over the Internet (as electronic mail). The client agrees to pay you in electronic money. As your bills become due, the client sends the money to you over the Internet, and it is downloaded into your computer. You, in turn, pay your bills by sending electronic cash from your computer and by loading up your smart card.

Only you—a smart New York lawyer—will decide what electronic and paper records to create and keep for this transaction; and anyone who can sell personal services over the Internet—be they lawyers, programmers, writers, architects, or engineers—will have the same capability.

In the digital age, it will be increasingly easy to move or create a financial portfolio anywhere in the world, and to do so anonymously and using encrypted transactions. The government can respond in two ways: It can try to know and control everything (the totalitarian response), or it can adapt its rules to the new reality (the libertarian or classical liberal response). A middle course is impossible since it would lead to ongoing corruption and civil struggle.

Eliminating the Reasons for Tax Evasion

An argument against financial privacy is that it will make the collection of some types of taxes more difficult for government. This is indeed true, but it is not enough to justify preventing financial privacy; in fact, it can be an argument for protecting financial privacy. When a government is unjust and corrupt, the people have both the right and the duty to oppose it. One form of opposition is the refusal to fund the government to the best of one's ability, which can take the form of deliberate tax avoidance or evasion.

The statutes of many countries, including the United States, make it illegal to fund or make payments to criminal organizations. But what if the government is the criminal organization? The National Socialist (Nazi) government under Adolf Hitler was, by any definition, a criminal organization. Many Germans, Jews, and others found a way to move their financial capital out of Germany to presumed safe havens. No one faults them now for evading Germany's taxes, because any tax receipts or financial assets confiscated by the Nazi government were bound to be used, at least in part, for immoral and corrupt purposes, including concentration camps and weapons of mass destruction.

The 20th century is littered with the skeletons of criminal governments funded by taxing their own citizens. The question of the right and moral course of action when one is confronted with a Hitler is easy, but what if one is confronted with a democratically elected government that is corrupt but not criminal in the Hitlerian sense?

For example, the District of Columbia government under Mayor Marion Barry was, by any reasonable definition, venal and incompetent. Residents of and visitors to Washington were faced with a police force that had a miserable success rate in solving crimes, a school system that spent far more than the national average per pupil and yet failed to provide many of its students with even a basic education, and a contracting system that rewarded friends of the mayor. Residents of such a jurisdiction see little return on their tax dollars and are inclined to develop elaborate schemes to evade paying taxes.

By contrast, suburban residents, such as those in Fairfax County, Virginia, are far less tempted to evade taxes. The county government is regarded as well-managed by government standards. Most county politicians are not in legal trouble. Services are not as efficient as they are in the private sector, but taxpayers do see some return on their money. The moral of the story: When people begin deciding for themselves which taxes to pay and not pay, the very institution of government is undermined.

To maintain a civilized society, it is important for people to believe that their units of government are honest and reasonably efficient. People who believe their government is corrupt will find moral justification to "opt out" of paying taxes if they think they can get away with it. The correct policy is to promote honest and efficient government, not more totalitarian tax enforcement.

The American experience demonstrates that most people will pay their taxes if, on balance, they believe the revenues collected will not be completely wasted. Thus, in the new digital age, it will be increasingly important for politicians to restore the honor system to the tax system, lower taxes, rein in the IRS, and spend the people's money wisely.

Tax reform is an important part of this strategy. We can only hope that our elected officials will choose this route. The other alternative—creating an ever more intrusive IRS that takes away even more of our freedoms—is too terrible to imagine.

Jack Faris is President and CEO of the National Federation of Independent Business (NFIB), the nation's largest small-business advocacy organization. He has led the NFIB since 1992, and frequently notes that he is drawing on his experiences in his family's service station business and owning a small business for 12 years. Recently named the fourth most powerful lobby in Washington by *Fortune* magazine, NFIB is leading a nationwide crusade to sunset the IRS tax code by December 31, 2000. More recently, Mr. Faris has led the battle to repeal the death tax.

4

TIME TO "SCRAP THE CODE"

Jack Faris
President and CEO
National Federation of Independent Business

The irony of the effort to implement tax reform is that, as proponents have grown more insistent, the tax code itself has simply grown. It is larger and more complex today than when flat tax reformers Robert Hall and Alvin Rabushka first offered their ideas to the world. So, while others may argue the relative merits of a flat income tax versus a national sales tax, I fear that this discussion assumes we already have won the battle.

Because of this, I have focused the attention of the National Federation of Independent Business (NFIB) on the real problem for America's small business owners—the current IRS tax code. Simply put, I believe real tax reform will not occur at the same time the IRS Code is being expanded and complicated even further. We need to abolish the current code first and then replace it with a code that eliminates confiscatory tax rates, encourages work and savings, is fair to all taxpayers, foregoes social engineering, contains no hidden taxes, and is difficult to change.

> *"If all income were taxed at the same rate, much of the perceived unfairness of the current system would be eradicated."*

In short—as NFIB says—we need to "Scrap the Code."

THE GROWING SUPPORT FOR SCRAPPING THE CODE

As I travel around the country and listen to small business owners, one fact becomes clear: The tax code is beyond repair. Small business owners know this better than most. For that reason, on September 22, 1997, in Independence, Missouri, NFIB launched a nationwide petition drive calling on the President and Congress to abolish the IRS Code by a date certain and offer the American people a simple and fair tax code that will reward work and savings.

The Campaign to Abolish the IRS Code outlined a series of steps—beginning with legislation that would sunset the IRS Code by a specific date and ending with Congress adopting a new tax code by July 4, 2001—to facilitate a national debate and a referendum to determine what America's tax code for the 21st century should be.

Following the "Scrap the Code" kickoff, NFIB designated April 15, 1997, as National "It's our Money, Not TheIRS!" Day. Volunteers and supporters were at designated post offices in more than 100 cities nationwide, collecting signatures for a petition asking Congress and the President to abolish the IRS Code and replace it with something better. Our goal was to remind taxpayers on tax filing day that the money they are sending to the government belongs to them, not to the IRS.

What began in September 1997 as a drive to collect a million signatures on a petition calling on Congress and the President to abolish the current IRS Code has grown rapidly into a nationwide movement focusing the country's attention on widespread IRS abuses and the need to change the nation's tax system.

We have had our share of successes. On June 17, 1998, a flatbed truck piled high with petitions sat in front of the U.S. Congress. After a rally calling for passage of legislation to sunset the current tax code as a first step toward implementing a fair and simple tax code, the House of Representatives passed the Tax Code Termination Act by a vote of 219 to 209.

On October 28, 1998, Lee Perry, a small business owner from San Diego, became the millionth person to sign the petition calling for a new tax code. Our grassroots effort had swept across the nation and gathered the million signatures in little more than a year.

But we also have had failures. Our legislation to sunset the IRS Code succeeded in the House in July but failed in the Senate later in the year, coming short of the 60 votes needed to overcome a procedural roadblock. Moreover, the elections last November may have reduced support for "Scrap the Code" in the House, leaving its prospects for adoption uncertain.

However, as we all saw with Steve Forbes' campaign in 1996, a single presidential candidate pushing a good idea can raise awareness of an issue that transcends the campaign itself. NFIB plans to make scrapping the code that sort of issue.

HOW THE TAX CODE TARGETS SMALL BUSINESS

Why are small businesses leading the charge to scrap the IRS Code? The answer is simple. Small businesses—more than any other segment of our economy—are a favorite target of the IRS Code and the Internal Revenue Service. When tax reformers raise the issues of tax code complexity and compliance costs, they usually talk about the burden placed on America's businesses.

Ordinary taxpayers are more fortunate by comparison. Most do not itemize. They receive their W-2 forms, take the standard deduction, and send in the 1040EZ. But as Chart 4.1 shows, small business owners find themselves buried under the most complex areas of the tax code, and while big corporations have the luxury of utilizing accounting offices and tax professionals,

Chart 4.1

Tax Code Complexity: Smaller Firms Face Significantly Higher Costs

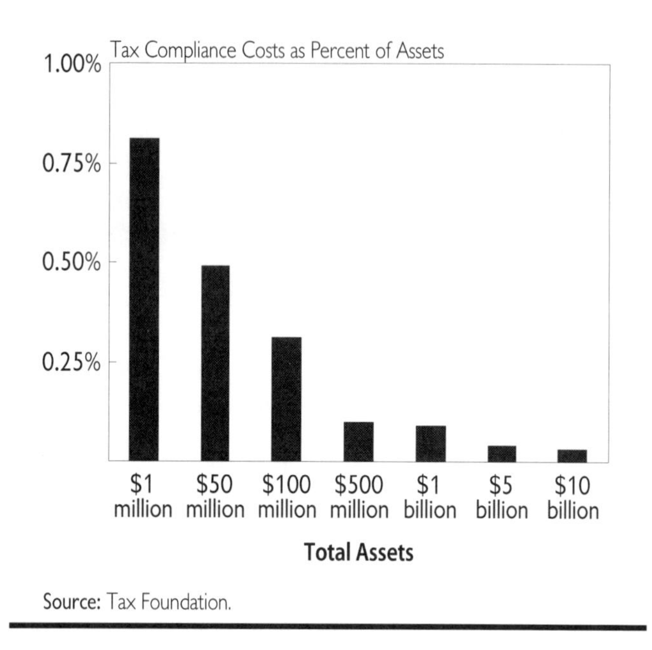

Source: Tax Foundation.

many small business owners must fill out and file their own returns.

Small businesses historically pay about one-tenth of the income tax revenues collected by the federal government. That was about $60 billion in 1994. But the total burden of the tax code on small businesses is much greater.

The Center for the Study of American Business has reported that small firms with fewer than 20 employees spent more than $5,000 per employee in 1992 to comply with federal regulations. Paperwork alone—mainly tax-related paperwork—cost these small firms more than $2,000 per employee, or twice as much per worker as the paperwork costs imposed on firms with 500 or more employees. Any way you look at it, America's small businesses shoulder the brunt of the tax code's complexity.

"Any way you look at it, America's small businesses shoulder the brunt of the tax code's complexity."

Why are small businesses affected so disproportionately? One reason is that the most complex parts of the tax code are targeted directly at small business owners.

The Alternative Minimum Tax

The individual alternative minimum tax (AMT) is a remarkably complex and obtuse provision in a tax code not known for its clarity. It literally requires taxpayers to calculate their taxes twice and then pay the larger amount.

Who did Congress have in mind when it created the AMT? America's small businesses. Of the AMT's 27 different adjustments and so-called tax preference items—deductions disallowed or reduced—16 are business-related. (Keep in mind that we are talking about the *individual* alternative minimum tax. Corporations have their own AMT.)

How complex is the AMT? Line 8 says, "Enter the difference between regular tax and AMT depreciation." This means that small business owners have to recalculate the value of their depreciation allowances using "the straight line method over 40 years with the same mid-month convention used for the regular tax," or the "straight line method over the property's class life with the same convention used for the regular tax," or the "150 percent declining balance method, switching to the straight line method for the first year it gives a larger tax deduction, over the property's class life"—depending, of course, on the type of property involved. And they have to do this calculation for every depreciable asset they own!

Understand? Neither do I. Moreover, there are 26 other adjustments needed to calculate AMT taxable income.

Worse, the AMT has the side effect of hitting taxpayers when they can least afford the bill. Businesses suffering from lower than expected revenues are more likely to fall into the clutches of the AMT than is a thriving business. The AMT, in effect, kicks small businesses when they are down. As your cash flow goes down, your AMT tax bite goes up.

The tax code is full of "AMTs," and adjustments like depreciation schedules, death taxes, and accounting methods fall heaviest on the individual entrepreneur with business-related income.

IRS Abuses

The IRS continually targets small business owners as part of its tax code enforcement effort. Just days after we launched our "Scrap the Code" campaign, the nation saw in televised hearings what small business owners have known for decades: The IRS has focused much of its abuse on small businesses and lower-income Americans—the very taxpayers who are least likely to mount a formidable legal defense.

The hearings before the Senate Finance Committee highlighted the abuse some IRS agents have inflicted on taxpayers. The committee heard, for example, from general contractor Tom Savage. The IRS held Tom liable for the unpaid taxes of one of his subcontractors. It harassed Tom and his business for months, illegally seized money that was owed to him, and eventually extorted $50,000 from him that both he and the IRS knew he did not owe. Tom settled because the legal fees necessary to win the case would have exceeded the settlement.

Congress also heard from Nancy Jacobs, who, together with her optometrist husband, was harassed by the IRS for 17 years because the IRS was using the wrong Employer Identification Number. At the time of the hearings, the IRS had admitted its mistake, but it still owed the Jacobses $26,000 in excess tax payments.

Finally, Congress heard testimony from actual IRS agents who stated unequivocally that the IRS targets taxpayers with fewer resources who are less likely to put up a fight over erroneous tax bills.

Although an IRS reform bill was passed by the 105th Congress and signed by the President, this solved only a small part of the problem. Both the burden of the tax code and the fear it inspires remain. The fear begins when the business owner looks at the tax forms to be filed for the first time. They are intimidating. Even when the forms are complete, there is a fear that mistakes were made unknowingly. And the greatest fear of all comes with a knock on the door, a letter, or a phone call from the IRS saying, in so many words, "You made a mistake, and now you must pay."

> *"Congress heard testimony from actual IRS agents who stated unequivocally that the IRS targets taxpayers with fewer resources who are less likely to put up a fight over erroneous tax bills."*

The "Scrap the Code" effort is not just an attempt to reduce these paperwork fears and paperwork expenses. It is also an attempt to restore a certain level of justice to our tax collection system. The Senate Finance Committee hearings provided ample, clear evidence that the current system is unjust. From witness after witness, day after day, Congress learned that the IRS uses the complexity of the IRS Code and the unlimited resources at its disposal to target America's small businesses unfairly.

WHY SCRAPPING THE CODE IS VITAL

Perhaps because of its successes, the "Scrap the Code" effort has incurred the wrath of a remarkable number of people. The President called the plan "irresponsible" and "reckless." Others have been even less kind. Nonetheless, scrapping the tax code will continue to be NFIB's top tax priority for the simple reason that it *is* responsible. NFIB's responses to the President's accusations are clear:

Is it "irresponsible" to sunset the IRS Code? Consider the proof from the states that the first step to dramatic and positive reform often begins by striking existing law.

- **In Wisconsin,** Governor Tommy Thompson teamed up with the legislature to redesign the state's welfare system. They began by sunsetting the existing welfare system. By doing so, they forced all sides to debate and review the issue and to write new legislation to replace the former system. The process worked so well for welfare reform that they used it to develop a new property tax system as well.
- **In Michigan,** Governor John Engler wanted to reduce property taxes and reconfigure how the state paid for public schools. He started by eliminating the existing property tax. That forced the legislature to examine ways to tax property owners and fund public education. Once again, the approach worked; Michigan's property owners enjoyed a 30 percent tax cut, and school funding across the state was made more equitable.

The bottom line is that striking old rules can be an essential first step toward improving a broken system. The sunset process works, and there is evidence from the states to prove it.

Is sunsetting the IRS Code "reckless"? Claims that sunsetting the IRS Code will cause disruption and havoc in the business community and on Wall Street are baseless. Scrapping the code would not add one ounce of uncertainty that does not already exist. Three years ago, the Joint Economic Committee reported that the tax on capital gains had been changed, on average, once every 24 months. Congress has altered the capital gains tax twice since then.

In fact, since Ronald Reagan took office in 1981, Congress has passed and the President has signed 15 major revisions of the tax code. We have had an ERTA, a TEFRA, a COBRA, several OBRAs, a TRA—and the acronyms go on and on. Congress knocks out a major tax bill just about every 14 months, and that figure does not include the dozens of tax bills, amendments, and proposals that either fail in Congress or are vetoed by the President.

> *"In fact, since... 1981, Congress has passed and the President has signed 15 major revisions of the tax code.... Congress knocks out a major tax bill just about every 14 months."*

There is an entire industry of lobbyists, writers, and well-heeled lawyers whose sole employment involves watching what is happening in the tax-writing committees in Congress and keeping their clients up-to-date on possible tax law changes. I guarantee that not one of them knows what the IRS Code will look like in 2002, whether we sunset the IRS Code or not.

Some critics charge that sunsetting the IRS Code will deprive the federal government of necessary revenues. This is an absurd argument. Under NFIB's proposal, the worst that can happen is that we end up with the existing federal tax code. The best that can happen, of course, is that we get a new tax code that encourages growth and job creation. Either way, taxpayers will have advance warnings of any changes being considered, just as they do today.

WHAT SHOULD THE NEW CODE LOOK LIKE?

Although NFIB is not promoting a specific replacement tax plan, I have presented Congress with the following "Seven Points of Principle" that it should consider when developing a new tax code that will be fair to small business. Specifically, a new tax code should:

- **Lower taxes**—to create jobs and opportunities.
- **Foster growth**—by encouraging work and savings.
- **Be fair**—for all taxpayers.
- **Be simple**—so all taxpayers can understand it.
- **Be neutral**—with no social engineering.
- **Be visible**—with no hidden taxes.
- **Be stable**—and difficult to change.

People have asked me to move beyond these principles and outline what sort of tax code small businesses would like to see. Here are some additional guidelines gleaned from my travels around the country, NFIB's polls of its members, and NFIB's Small Business Summit last summer:

1. **Reduce the overall tax burden.**

   Any discussion of tax reform should be held within the context of an overall tax cut. Revenue neutrality destroyed whatever benefits may have been derived from the 1986 Tax Reform Act. We should learn our lesson and not be shackled into thinking we have to raise Peter's taxes to cut Paul's. By embracing a tax cut as part of reform, we can minimize the concerns raised about winners and losers.

   Moreover, making tax cuts an integral part of tax reform strengthens rather than weakens the proposal. The current tax burden is at an all-time high. Considering that we are in the midst of 30 years of relative peace, that statistic alone is a compelling argument for tax cuts. If our ultimate goal is leaner, more efficient government, then cutting the tax burden should be our first priority.

Chart 4.2

Taxes Now Consume Record Share of Economy's Output

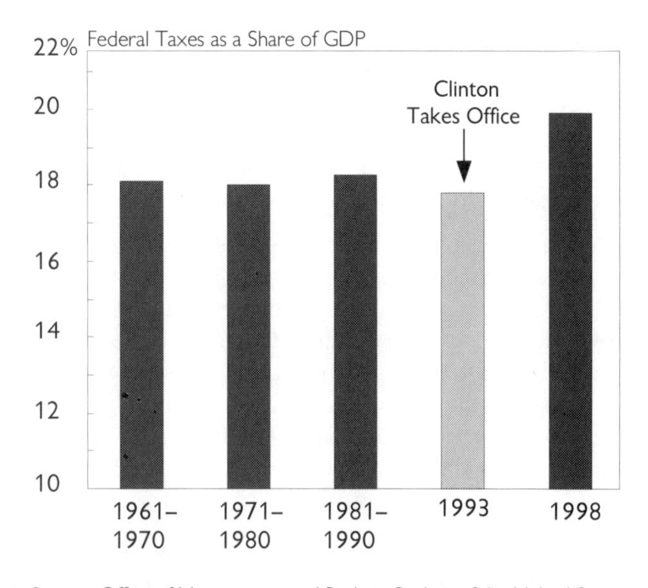

Source: Office of Management and Budget, *Budget of the United States Government, FY1999.*

2. **Tax income at one low rate.**

   Tax reform without a single, unified tax rate is no tax reform at all. Representative Richard Gephardt (D–MO) has proposed a so-called flat tax with five rates that fails to address the most basic complaints regarding the current tax code. If we are going to discuss tax reform seriously, a single low rate must be one of the underlying principles.

   This principle addresses the two fundamental problems of unfairness and complexity. If all income were taxed at the same rate, much of the perceived unfairness of the current system would be eradicated; at the same time, distinctions between types of income—labor, capital, and business—would disappear, making the code much less complex.

3. **Tax income only once.**

When tax reformers talk about "fostering growth" through the tax code, they really mean reducing the current overtaxation of investment and savings. Right now, the tax code is biased against savings and investment because it taxes capital income two or three times.

Solving this problem promotes both growth and simplicity. Taxing income once means eliminating death taxes. That reform alone would make a dramatic improvement by reducing tax code complexity and raising economic growth. It also means eliminating the double taxation of interest and dividends. There is overwhelming evidence regarding the negative relationship between taxes on savings and investment and economic growth. As taxes on savings go up, economic growth goes down.

When NFIB asked its members, "Should the tax system be changed to encourage savings and discourage consumption?" more than three-fourths replied "Yes." Small businesses understand the importance of encouraging savings and investment.

4. **Be visible to all taxpayers.**

This is an "anti-VAT" principle, pure and simple. The value-added tax (VAT) is uniformly despised by small businesses because it is a hidden tax. They have seen the damage the VAT has done in Canada and Europe, and they fear the same results here in America.

Back in 1985, we asked our members, "Do you favor or oppose creation of a value-added tax as a replacement for the current income tax system?" Six out of ten said "No."

> Our members voted against the VAT because they fear it would be used to supplement, rather than replace, the current income tax code. I believe the case against the VAT has strengthened since then.

CONCLUSION

"Reckless" and "irresponsible" are the words President Clinton used to describe our plan to abolish the IRS tax code. With all due respect to the President, what is truly irresponsible is a tax code that is anti-work, anti-savings, and anti-family. What is reckless is continuing to live with a tax code of seven million words that sucks the life right out of our economy.

President Clinton even indicated that small business owners want to create "fiscal anarchy" by scrapping the code and then figuring out what to do next. But small employers understand that sometimes the old law must be laid to rest before a new law can take its place. By attacking our plan, the President has insulted thousands of small business owners who have joined NFIB's Campaign to Abolish the IRS Code and have signed petitions calling for the abolition of the current tax code.

This campaign for responsible tax reform is a grassroots effort to mobilize small business owners and supporters to call upon the President and Congress to abolish the IRS Code and to replace it with a simple and fair tax code that rewards work and savings. Since our petition drive began, five simple words have become a declaration of independence for small business: "It's our Money, Not TheIRS!"

Instead of stubbornly embracing the status quo, President Clinton should join the campaign to "Scrap the Code," and even champion the cause. If the President listens to small business on this one issue, he will be remembered as the President who set this country's tax code on track to ensure that the 21st century is the *real* American Century.

Doug Bandow is a Senior Fellow at the Cato Institute. After working in Ronald Reagan's presidential campaign in 1980, he served as Special Assistant to President Reagan and Deputy Director for Legal Affairs for the Office of Policy Development in the Reagan Administration. A provocative, incisive observer of current events, he writes a weekly column carried regularly by *The Detroit News*, *The Orange County Register*, *The San Diego Union*, and *The Washington Times*. He also contributes to *Christianity Today*, *Tabletalk*, and *World*. A recipient of the Amy Award for religious writing, Mr. Bandow has authored *Beyond Good Intentions: A Biblical View of Politics* and *The Politics of Plunder: Misgovernment in Washington.* He holds a B.S. in economics from Florida State University and a J.D. degree from the Stanford University Law School.

5

A MORAL TAX CODE IS FAIR AND SIMPLE

Doug Bandow
Senior Fellow, The Cato Institute

Liberals and conservatives, Democrats and Republicans alike try to claim the moral high ground when it comes to taxation. But deriving moral principles of right and wrong and applying them to politics—let alone taxation—is not easy. When it comes to morality, many people believe they will "know it when they see it," but that attitude is too vague to spark meaningful debate. The problem, of course, is that "fairness" invariably is in the eye of the beholder.

Perhaps the best definition of fairness is that the law treats everyone equally. This principle was artfully expressed by Will Rogers, who noted that "People want just taxes more than they want lower taxes. They want to know that every man is paying his proportionate share according to his wealth." Steve Forbes could not have said it any better.

Some interpret "fair" to mean high and progressive taxes that redistribute income through all manner of social programs. Yet such a system of coercive income redistribution lacks a moral basis. Unchecked, the government will continue to take more in taxes because the money is there to be taken, regardless of the suffering it causes the taxpayer. To be fair and moral, tax rates must be simple, low, and equal, administered by a strictly limited government, and enforced non-intrusively.

PHILOSOPHICAL ROOTS OF EQUALITY BEFORE THE LAW

Unequal application of the law not only violates the Constitution's promise of equal treatment, but also mocks the philosophical heritage upon which our nation was founded.

Respect for the rule of law—and equality before the law—is an integral part of Western civilization. Aristotle noted that fairly administered laws protect against individual whims; thus, "it is more proper that the law should govern than any of the citizens." But these laws were to be applied fairly. Indeed, the ancient Greeks had a term, *isonomia*, which captured the principle of "equality of laws to all manner of persons." Solon, renowned as the lawgiver in ancient Athens, established a system rooted in the concept of "equal laws for the noble and the base." In other words, the powerful could not benefit from special treatment.

"Unequal application of the law not only violates the Constitution's promise of equal treatment, but also mocks the philosophical heritage upon which our nation was founded."

The Romans continued this tradition. The Laws of the Twelve Tables state that "no privileges, or statutes shall be enacted in favour of private persons, to the injury of others contrary to the law common to all citizens, and which individuals, no matter of what rank, have a right to make use of."

Of course, neither the Greeks nor the Romans complied fully with these principles, but this does not detract from their accomplishment. With the collapse of the Roman Empire, Europe entered the Dark Ages and the rule of law was replaced by absolutism. It was not until the 1600s that the tradition of equal treatment revived, and England was the nation that led the way.

Eventually, a new philosophical tradition developed, one that reasserted the principle that laws apply evenly to the population. John Locke wrote that "Freedom of men under government is to have a standing rule to live by, common to every one of that society." And Blackstone wrote that law is "something permanent, uniform, and universal." Nobel laureate Friedrich von Hayek summed up the issue by noting that "The great aim of the struggle for liberty has been equality before the law."

Applied to the issue of taxes, these principles indicate clearly that the ideal tax code is one that does not discriminate among citizens. Voltaire concurred, writing that, "In the matter of taxation, every privilege is an injustice." Scottish philosopher John McCulloch was even more direct: "The moment you abandon…the cardinal principle of exacting from all individuals the same proportion of their income…you are at sea without rudder or compass, and there is no amount of injustice or folly you may not commit."

Unfortunately, the wisdom of these philosophers was soon forgotten. The progressive tax enjoyed its modern birth in Prussia. According to Hayek, this led German scholar Rudolf von Gneist to decry the abandonment "of the most sacred principle of equality." England and America followed shortly thereafter, yet scholars in the English-speaking world were equally repelled by progressive taxation. Renowned philosopher John Stuart Mill described progression as "a mild form of robbery" and referred to envy as "the most anti-social and evil of all passions."

THE RELIGIOUS ROOTS OF LIMITED GOVERNMENT

The fundamental principles of fairness also have their roots in the moral code of the Founding Fathers, who in turn were influenced by their faith. Their faith offered the Framers of the Constitution general principles by which to shape a moral fiscal code. Although these principles do not predetermine a particular form or level of taxation, they do suggest the direction in which prudent policymakers should move.

There is an undercurrent in both Jewish and Christian scripture which suggests that government's power should be limited, since government is an institution established by humans, and "man," as a fallen creature, is all too willing to do wrong. As historical experiences in the Bible demonstrate, those who are evil are particularly adept at taking control of governments.

As Jeremiah of the Old Testament warned, people are skilled in doing evil. Such people are precisely the ones most likely to run political systems, and they are able to do more evil with the greater authority of government behind them. Frequently, they use their coercive power to tax to do evil. The author of Ecclesiastes warns that power is "on the side of their oppressors." (Ecclesiastes 4:1) Whatever form of government is chosen, there is clear teaching in Judeo-Christian Old Testament scripture against the arbitrary use of political power.

The teaching of the New Testament, though less direct, is consistent. For instance, Jesus Christ regularly denounced the ruling religious establishment for what clearly was an abuse of its otherwise apparently proper authority. He told a parable about an unjust judge "who neither feared God nor cared about men." (Luke 18:2) He expected His disciples to be different from "the rulers of the Gentiles," who "lord it over them, and their high officials" who "exercise authority over them." (Matthew 20:25)

Although Jewish and Christian scriptures alike evince a particular concern over justice for the powerless, biblical justice requires impartial treatment of the rich as well. For instance, God commanded the ancient Israelites, "do not pervert justice; do not show partiality to the poor or favoritism to the great, but judge your neighbor fairly." (Leviticus 19:15)

Respect for Civil Society. If anything is clear from Jewish and Christian religious traditions, it is that politics is not everything. Indeed, politics is not much at all. More important is the preservation of a sufficiently large and vibrant civil sector in which people can be salt and light, in Christ's words, by carrying on their daily lives. This may seem trivial, but it is not. As James asked, "What good is it, my brothers, if a man claims to have faith but has no deeds?" (James 2:14) That outworking of one's faith is an important aspect of one's spiritual walk.

Indeed, Christ's description of the accursed on Judgment Day makes little sense unless people are capable of exercising control over a substantial share of their own resources: "I was hungry and you gave me nothing to eat, I was thirsty and you gave me nothing to drink, I was a stranger and you did not invite me in, I was naked and you did not clothe me, I was sick and in prison and you did not look after me." (Matthew 25:42–43) None of this is possible in a world in which most resources are controlled collectively and politically.

Particularly important is the preservation of other institutions that, like government, are ordained of God. The New Testament devotes far more attention to the issues of family responsibility and relationships and church teaching and activities than it does to politics. It is within family and church that the most important functions—worship of God, proclamation of the Gospel, care for the needy, moral education of the community, upbringing of the young—are handled. The importance of these institutions actually may have expanded over the ages as religious orders formed economic enterprises, founded universities, and maintained hospitals.

The Apostle Paul and his fellow church leaders largely ignored political issues, other than declaring a general duty to obey and pray for government officials. First, politics was less important than most other aspects of life. Second, politics in practice played a much smaller role in society. For most people, especially those living in peaceful segments of the Roman Empire, contact with government was limited largely to the collection of taxes. The state, as such, did not attempt to regulate and manipulate virtually every aspect of people's lives as it does today.

Limited Tax Rates. Of course, one must be careful when attempting to apply general scriptural principles to modern policy. Presumably, even 40 percent tax levies today are easier to bear than the 10 percent tithe to the king denounced by Samuel in the Old Testament, because modern man is far wealthier. Nevertheless, there is a moral argument for keeping as much wealth as possible in individual hands.

Excessive state exactions prevent people from fulfilling a number of important duties. One is to give to God. The ancient Hebrews were expected not just to tithe, but to make a number of different offerings. Generous giving was noteworthy in the early Christian church as well; in Jerusalem, people often would turn over entire properties to the church. Explained the Apostle Paul, "God loves a cheerful giver." (2 Corinthians 9:7)

Another high duty is to care for one's family. Family members are to act as the first line of assistance for extended family members, such as widows. Charity is supposed to be a voluntary response, not only to the need of one's family, but also to members of the church and the larger community. Such giving is impossible if the government is confiscating too much of people's incomes, whether or not that money is directed formally toward the poor.

Fair and Not Confiscatory. For all of today's highly politicized discussion about greed, neither Jewish nor Christian scriptures treat that vice among the top concerns. Of course, materialist lusts can block the path to salvation: Christ warned about the difficulty of the rich entering the kingdom of heaven. Indeed, the Apostle Paul taught that "the love of money is the root of all evil." (1 Timothy 6:10)

More destructive, however, is the related sin of envy. Both reflect a love of "the world," as the Apostle John put it, which interferes with the relationship with God. (1 John 2:15) But envy has important implications for the larger social order. Greedy people tend to mess up their own lives. The covetous harm other people as well. The Tenth Commandment is clear: "You shall not covet your neighbor's house. You shall not covet your neighbor's wife, or his manservant or maidservant, his ox or donkey, or anything that belongs to your neighbor." (Exodus 20:17)

In short, both the greedy and the envious allow material desires to interfere with personal spiritual development. But the greedy usually satisfy their wishes by harmless, indeed often socially beneficial, means—working harder, inventing new products, developing new services, and so on. The truly covetous are happy only if they are able to harm their neighbor by taking something from him or her. The easiest way to do so, other than to use a sword or gun to heist someone's wallet, is to use political power.

The Importance of Prosperity. The God of the Bible is not concerned primarily about people making money; He is far more concerned about getting them into a right relationship with Him. However, prosperity, so long as it does not interfere with one's spiritual walk—as it did with the rich young man in the New Testament, for instance—is generally a good thing. God promised the Hebrew nation that He would bless it materially if it followed His precepts. The Proverbs are full of practical guidance on how to prosper.

In the New Testament, Christ enjoyed the fellowship of the wealthy, though He enjoined them to keep their focus on spiritual matters. And the early Christian church relied on richer members to help care for the poor. Those with more income were expected to help those in need, but there was nothing wrong in their accumulation of property. Without such accumulations, in fact, how could believers take care of those around them, including "all people"? (Galatians 6:10)

HOW PROGRESSIVE TAX RATES PROMOTE CLASS WARFARE

The progressive income tax has become an icon for some, but no principle of justice warrants seizing a steadily increasing share of people's earnings. So long as people's wealth is earned legitimately, they should not be penalized simply because they are better off. Indeed, rising marginal tax rates punish people who are contributing the most economically to society.

It is hard to view progressivity as anything but a tool of envy. Shortly after taking office, President Clinton announced, "Before I ask working Americans to work harder and pay more, I will ask the economic elite who made more money and paid less in taxes to pay their fair share." Senator James Sasser (D–TN), then chairman of the Senate Budget Committee, wanted to raise top marginal rates because, he complained, Ronald Reagan's 1981 tax cut "distributed its benefits disproportionately among the rich and the very rich."

Such rhetoric carries over into the popular media. One *U.S. News & World Report* headline intoned, "It'll just hurt a little." The subhead went on, "Most taxpayers can relax. In the end, only the rich get soaked." *The New York Times* reported, "Democrats Hail House Proposal Taxing the Rich."

Such arguments are simple demagoguery. The Reagan tax cuts, an across-the-board 25 percent rate reduction, provided more in tax relief to the wealthy because *the wealthy were paying so much more in taxes*. It would seem to be simple fairness to provide someone who paid, say, ten times as much in taxes with ten times as much in tax relief.

In fact, the latest IRS data (for 1996) show that the top 1 percent of earners currently pay about 30 percent of all income taxes, up from 25 percent a decade before. The top 5 percent pay more than half; the top 10 percent pay more than three-fifths; and the top 25 percent pay more than four-fifths, or four out of every five tax dollars. All of these shares are up from 1986. The portion paid by top earners started rising in 1981, when President Reagan pushed major tax rate cuts through Congress.

Progressivity is, of course, routinely cited as a mechanism to ensure greater income equality. However, so long as one's money is earned justly, there is no moral cause for forcibly seizing wealth from one person to hand off to another just to make the income statistics look more "fair."

Moreover, the progressive income tax appears to be relatively ineffective as a tool of redistribution. Although President Clinton pushed one of the largest tax hikes in history through Congress, economist Bruce Bartlett wrote in *The Washington Times* in October 1998 that "the rich have gotten richer faster during the Clinton administration than at any time in history."

At some point, higher marginal rates become clearly self-defeating. History indicates that the revenue-maximizing rate is less than 30 percent. Above that level, collections are diminished as people adjust their behavior: People spend significant resources on tax avoidance activities, wasting money in order to shelter a little more from the tax man; incur the risk of illegally hiding income; and/or work and invest less, preferring to consume, often conspicuously. Such effects are most obvious at confiscatory tax levels; purchasing a small plane or a Rolls Royce is relatively cheap if most of the return on an alternative use of the money—for example, as an investment—is taxed away.

"It is hard to view progressivity as anything but a tool of envy."

In this way, high rates bias taxpayers away from productive activities that otherwise would benefit everyone in society.

Chart 5.1

Rich Not Paying Their Share? Top 10% of Taxpayers Pay 60% of the Income Tax Burden

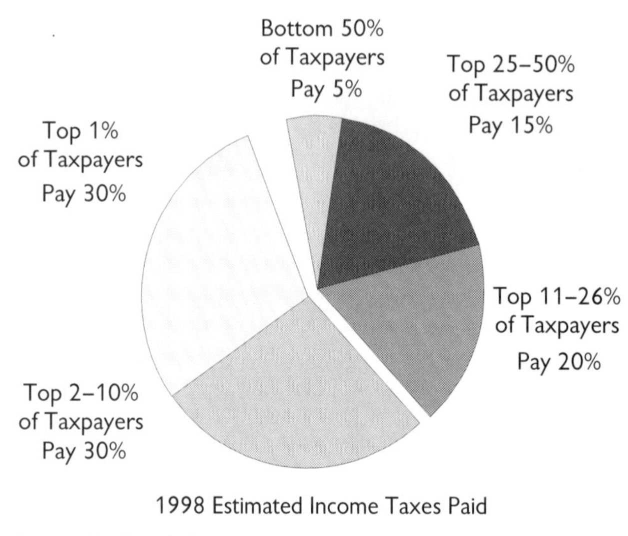

1998 Estimated Income Taxes Paid

Source: Tax Foundation.

According to a study for the National Center for Policy Analysis, Americans with incomes of over $1 million derive 75 percent of their income from investments, while those earning $200,000 a year or more receive 60 percent of their income from investments. Such large, investment-based earnings may seem scandalous to the envious, but this is the source of capital needed to create the jobs that employ low- and middle-income Americans.

Indeed, anyone seriously interested in the plight of the poor should be more concerned about expanding the nation's economic pie than with stealing additional funds from those who are financially successful. As the Organization for Economic Cooperation and Development observed a decade ago, "The income tax system is certainly a less effective tool for achieving equitable income distribution than are full employment and well-functioning social policies." Notable is the fact that the most incentive-minded President before Ronald Reagan was John F. Kennedy, whose proposal to lower rates across the board, passed after his death, helped spark the economic boom of the 1960s.

"[S]o long as one's money is earned justly, there is no moral cause for forcibly seizing wealth from one person to hand off to another just to make the income statistics look more 'fair.'"

Finally, progressivity creates a host of practical problems. Taxpayers have an incentive to transform income into different forms and to shift income over time. Even some advocates of the progressive income tax recognize the resulting weakness of their case. "With a flat tax it is a matter of indifference what the taxable unit is," explain Walter Blum and Harry Kalven in *The Uneasy Case for Progressive Taxation.* "But under a progressive system this issue poses an almost insuperably difficult problem of equity among taxpayers." It also distorts economic decision-making, causing people to make important business and investment decisions for tax rather than economic purposes.

A MORAL TAX CODE

The current tax system would not seem to be well-rooted in moral, and especially in biblical, precepts. Indeed, the current tax code violates all of the major scriptural principles that offer some guidance for building a responsible system of public finance. The federal government has become a Leviathan state, underwritten by the virtually limitless revenue available

Chart 5.2

Taxes Now Consume Record Share of Peacetime Economy

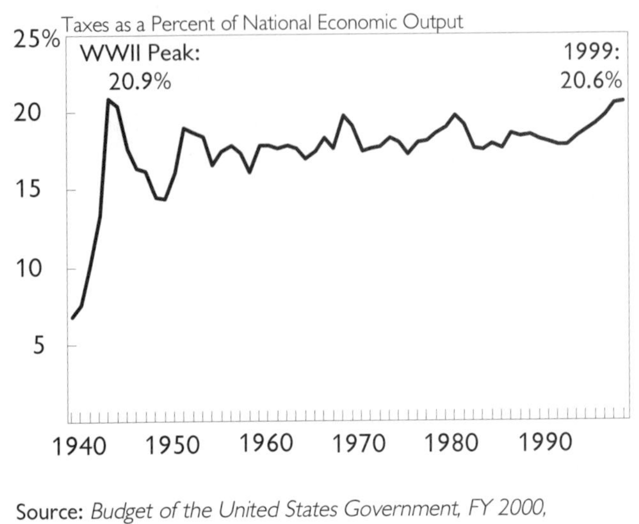

Source: *Budget of the United States Government, FY 2000,* Historical Tables.

through the progressive income tax. Taxes now consume a record share of the peacetime economy. It has turned into the avaricious creature foreseen by the prophet Samuel and may well be turning into the suffocating, arrogant, and tyrannical system envisioned by the Apostle John in Revelation. The IRS, in particular, has demonstrated how power can be abused.

Excessive tax rates inhibit the vibrant, nonpolitical community that was so important throughout biblical times and which is so critical for the cultivation of moral values today. At the same time, progressivity has encouraged envy-based politics, which poisons political debate. The combination of high rates and excessive complexity inhibits economic growth. Although the wealthy obviously would benefit from faster growth, they can survive handily if things stay the way they are. Prosperity is relatively more important to the poor who most need new, better, and higher-paying jobs in an expanding economy.

Former IRS Commissioner Fred Goldberg was right in arguing that tax reform is "the only way to liberate the American people from a system that is grotesquely burdensome and monstrous." But the right reform—a simple flat-rate tax—is critical.

Either a national sales tax or a flat tax would work. A simple flat-rate tax would make the full tax burden obvious to the public, allowing citizens to see and balance the full costs and benefits of government programs; and because all would share equally in paying for government, politicians would be prevented from playing the destructive and dishonest politics of envy. These factors alone likely would limit the growth of government to one that is more consistent with a free and virtuous society—one in which people are able to act as independent moral agents and practice their faith through wide-ranging nonpolitical interaction with their neighbors.

A simple flat-rate tax would treat everyone equally. This equal treatment would mean that the wealthy pay more, but in proportion to their increased resources—you earn ten times as much, you pay ten times as much in taxes. Foreclosing appeals to envy would help preserve justice; it would prevent demagogues from exploiting economic divisions and social engineers from manipulating people's behavior.

A simple flat-rate tax also would limit the potential for abusive legislation and enforcement practices. Politicians no longer would be able to sell special exemptions and other tax favors; unscrupulous IRS agents no longer would be able to prey upon innocent citizens and pry into their personal affairs; members of the public and government alike could spend their time and money on more productive activities.

Chart 5.3

Taxes Rise as Income Rises: All Taxpayers Are Treated Equally with a Flat Tax

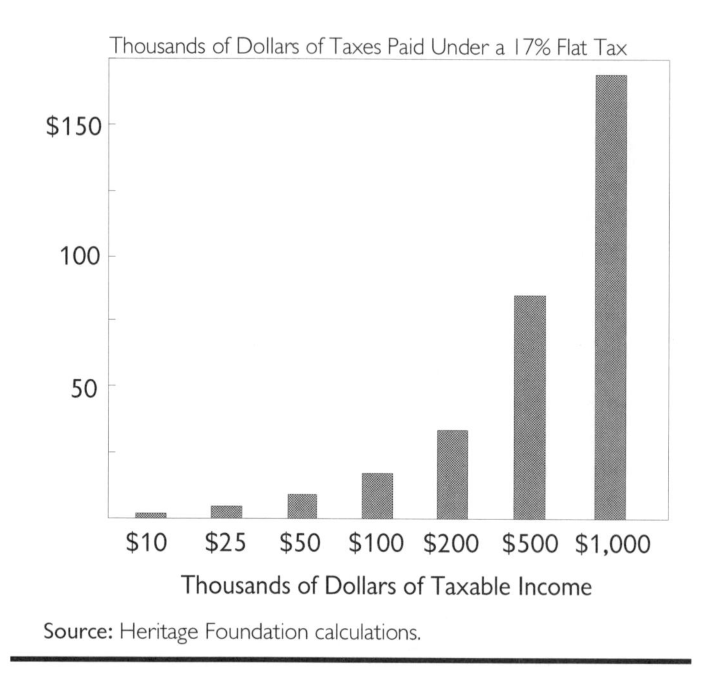

Source: Heritage Foundation calculations.

By lowering enforcement costs as well as eliminating the manifold economic distortions caused by a system characterized by high rates, inane requirements, and inordinate complexity, a simple flat-rate tax would spur economic growth. The new jobs and higher salaries generated by this growth would most help those at the bottom of the economic ladder.

CONCLUSION

Everyone says they want a fair tax system, but what many political activists mean by "fair" is a system with higher rates for anyone making more than themselves.

In fact, basic moral American principles, rooted in the Jewish and Christian faiths, point in another direction. Although any number of taxes and rates are consistent with these faiths, scripture demonstrates a wariness of expansive political power that can be abused so easily by sinful man.

Jewish and Christian teaching also emphasizes the importance of civil society as the primary arena through which people cooperate with one another, meet the needs of the less fortunate, and live their faiths. In particular, the Bible—which shaped the world view of the Founders—emphasizes the importance of justice for any minority that may be vulnerable to oppression.

For all of these reasons, a simple flat-rate tax would be not only fair, but significantly fairer than the present system. The wisdom with which God generously endows us, according to James 1:5, and upon which we are to rely in working with one another points in the same direction. In this case, at least, administrative simplicity and economic equality would prove to be both moral and smart.

Daniel J. Mitchell, McKenna Senior Fellow in Political Economy at The Heritage Foundation, is one of the nation's leading experts on the flat tax. For more than three years, he co-hosted the morning show on NET, the Political NewsTalk Network. Before joining The Heritage Foundation in 1990, Mr. Mitchell served as an economist for Senator Bob Packwood of Oregon. He also covered the Federal Reserve System for the Bush/Quayle transition team and was Director of Tax and Budget Policy for Citizens for a Sound Economy. He is the author of *The Flat Tax: Fairness, Jobs, and Growth*; his work also has been published in *The Wall Street Journal, The New York Times, National Review, The Villanova Law Review, The Journal of Regulation and Social Cost, USA Today,* and *Investor's Business Daily.* Mr. Mitchell received his B.A. and M.A. degrees in economics from the University of Georgia.

6

MAKE TAXES SIMPLE AND FAIR: ENACT THE FLAT TAX

Daniel J. Mitchell
McKenna Senior Fellow in Economic Policy
The Heritage Foundation

In 1997, *Money* magazine published a shocking story that demonstrated how our tax system has become an incomprehensible mess. *Money* gave tax information for a hypothetical family to professional tax preparers and asked them to fill out a tax return. Of the 45 responses received, not a single "expert" calculated the correct tax. No two of these professionals even came up with the same answer. Three-fourths of the responses missed the right answer by more than $1,000.

Unfortunately, this stunning revelation of the tax code's complexity had no effect on politicians. Later that year, Congress and the White House put together a tax package that could have been called the "Tax Lawyers' Full Employment and Accountants' Enrichment Act of 1997." This one law added 285 new sections to the tax law and amended more than 800 others. The number of lines in the form used for paying capital gains taxes, to cite just one example, more than doubled.

As a result, when *Money* repeated its tax test in 1998, the results were even more amazing. This time, it received 46 answers. Once again, however, all the answers were wrong and no two were identical. The response that was closest to the right answer (assuming the magazine's panel of experts had the right answer) was wrong by $610—in favor of the Internal Revenue Service. All told, there was a difference of $34,672 between the lowest and highest answers.

This is not to say that these accountants and other tax experts were stupid. Indeed, when *Money* sent its reporters to IRS customer service centers back in 1997 with a list of questions, they received the wrong answer 40 percent of the time. Moreover, adding further insult to injury, taxpayers who rely on inaccurate IRS information when filling out their tax returns are subject to full civil and criminal penalties. Unlike alleged murderers, rapists, and burglars, taxpayers who are accused by the IRS of wrongdoing have no constitutional rights. They are assumed guilty until they prove themselves innocent.

"With 569 separate forms and 17,000 pages of laws and regulations, the current code is a tangled mess that invites errors, evasion, and abuse."

America's tax system is a disgrace and an outrage. With 569 separate forms and 17,000 pages of laws and regulations, the current code is a tangled mess that invites errors, evasion, and abuse. Special-interest groups benefit the most from this complexity and use their political influence to create loopholes.

The big losers are ordinary taxpayers and small business owners—hard-working people who cannot afford high-priced lawyers, lobbyists, and accountants to help them wade through the ever-changing forms and regulations. This is why millions of middle-class taxpayers are subject to punitive tax rates; it is also why so much of what they save is expropriated by multiple layers of taxation.

The Internal Revenue Service makes this bad situation even worse. Because the tax laws are so confusing and contradictory, politicians have given the IRS immense powers of enforcement. Yet studies show that IRS agents often are just as baffled by the code as the rest of us are. The IRS charges tens of millions of taxpayers with mistakes every year, and about half of those accusations turn out to be false. The mistakes that are real are almost always the result of unintentional errors made by honest taxpayers and tax preparers.

As if these reasons were not enough to justify fixing the tax code, the most compelling reason is that doing so would help the less fortunate. People on the lower rungs of the economic ladder have the most to gain if the economy prospers—and the most to lose if the economy stumbles. A young family struggling from paycheck to paycheck, an inner-city worker seeking to realize the American dream, an entrepreneur risking everything to start a small business, a divorced woman getting back on her feet—these are the people that policymakers should keep in mind when they tackle the income tax code.

Fundamental reform is the only way to get rid of the current system and create a tax that is simple and fair for all Americans.

IT'S TIME TO START OVER

In many ways, we Americans are lucky. Our tax burden is not as onerous as the tax burden in many other nations. Yet the fact that other nations have tax codes that are worse than ours is no justification for maintaining the status quo. Our tax system is hopelessly unfair and lacks any moral authority. It is hostile to growth and mocks the principles of free enterprise and entrepreneurship that have served our country so well.

It is time to repeal the code and start over.

Discussing all of the reasons why our tax code should be scrapped requires an entire book—to which the other chapters in this volume attest. The major arguments for fundamental tax reform recur throughout these pages. Some of the problems discussed are based on economics and some are based on morality, but the tax code's key problems can be summarized as follows:

- **Discrimination.** The current tax code violates the Constitution's promise that all citizens will be treated equally. Some taxpayers, often thanks to special political connections and power, pay almost no tax. Others pay far too much tax. This undermines the basis of a free society.
- **Complexity.** Because of the incredible number of forms, regulations, and IRS rulings, many Americans pay professionals to fill out their tax forms. Yet, as so clearly demonstrated by the *Money* magazine surveys, even the experts make mistakes. The blame belongs to the politicians who have enacted more than 11,000 changes in various parts of the tax code since 1981.
- **High tax rates.** Under the present tax code, a successful entrepreneur will pay more than 40 cents of each additional dollar earned to the federal government. This burden can rise to over 50 cents when state income taxes are included, and more than 80 cents when estate taxes are added. These excessive rates penalize productive economic behavior and reduce incentives to work, create wealth, and take risks.
- **Multiple taxation.** Some forms of income, particularly from savings and investment, are subject to as many as four layers of tax. For example, a dollar of business income could be subject to corporate income taxes, personal income taxes, capital gains taxes, and estate taxes. This combined burden becomes confiscatory and undermines incentives to save and invest.
- **Social engineering.** Politicians have turned the tax code into a bewildering labyrinth of special preferences, penalties, and deductions that encourage certain types of behavior. Some income is taxed more than once, while other income is not taxed at all. Such complexity is the inevitable byproduct of a tax system that rewards those who can afford expensive law-

yers and accountants and that allows lawmakers to micromanage the economy.

- **Corruption.** For perfectly understandable reasons, taxpayers want to pay as little of their income to the government as possible. The current tax system allows well-connected and powerful groups to achieve this goal by creating special loopholes, many of which are a payoff for generous campaign contributions. Politicians benefit from this sordid practice while average taxpayers are squeezed to make up the shortfall.

The congressional IRS hearings in 1997 brought many of these problems sharply into focus. But they share an underlying common denominator which may be the most important reason to scrap the current system: As Doug Bandow explains elsewhere in this book, the Internal Revenue Code is immoral. The tax system lacks equality, fairness, and simplicity—features that must be fundamental to reform.

Many Americans look to Congress to create a tax code that no longer punishes hard-working families or entrepreneurs for creating wealth. They look forward to a new system that removes barriers to upward mobility. And they clearly want a tax code that strips the IRS of its abusive powers.

NEEDED: ONE TAX RATE, ONE SIMPLE FORM

Several intriguing tax reform proposals are being discussed on Capitol Hill and across America today, including a national sales tax. But the best-known and most popular is the flat tax. Why? Because everyone can understand the flat tax. Its guiding principle is equality: *All taxpayers will play by the same rules*, with no special loopholes and no special penalties.

In short, if Taxpayer A earns 100 times as much as Taxpayer B earns, he will pay 100 times more in taxes. This is simple, and it is fair. Equality is a guiding principle that should apply to taxes just as it does to individual rights.

Chart 6.1

A Simple Tax Form for Individuals

Form 1 | **Individual Wage Tax** | **1999**

Your first name and initial (if joint return, also give spouse's name and initial)	Last name	Your social security number
Home address (number and street including apartment number or rural route)		Spouse's social security number
City, town, or post office, state and ZIP code	Your occupation	
	Spouse's occupation	

1	Wages and salary and Pensions	1	
2	Personal allowance		
	(a) $23,200 for married filing jointly	2(a)	
	(b) $11,600 for single	2(b)	
	(c) $14,850 for single head of household	2(c)	
3	Number of dependents, not including spouse	3	
4	Personal allowances for dependents *(line 3 multiplied by $5,300)*	4	
5	Total personal allowances *(line 2 plus line 4)*	5	
6	Taxable wages *(line 1 less line 5, if positive: otherwise zero)*	6	
7	Tax *(17% of line 6)*	7	
8	Tax already paid	8	
9	Tax due *(line 7 less line 8, if positive)*	9	
10	Refund due *(line 8 less line 7, if positive)*	10	

Source: Office of Representative Richard Armey.

The postcard-size forms shown in this chapter illustrate how filing taxes will be far easier for both individuals and businesses under a flat tax. Unlike the current code's intrusive demands for information, you need to know only the size of your family and the amount of income you earned (a figure readily available to most Americans on the W-2 forms sent out by employers). Complying with this type of tax code requires almost no effort or uncertainty.

GUIDING PRINCIPLES OF THE FLAT TAX

1. *One low rate.*
2. *No double taxation of savings and investment.*
3. *Simplicity and transparency.*
4. *Equality and fairness.*
5. *No loopholes.*

The family allowance is another feature that will make the flat tax fair. Every taxpayer would receive a generous allowance based on family size, and would pay 17 percent on all income over that amount. In other words, the complexity that breeds confusion and fosters tax evasion today would disappear under the flat tax. The simple forms would eliminate virtually every source of conflict between taxpayers and the Internal Revenue Service.

The flat tax also eliminates the unfair way that the government double taxes savings and investment. Once income is earned and the tax paid, the IRS no longer has any reason to track how you use what remains so that it can tax what you save and invest a second time. The flat tax prevents the government from taking more than one bite of your income apple.

The flat tax is both good news and bad news for the rich. Honest, successful entrepreneurs will like the flat tax, since the rate will be low and savings and investment will not be double taxed. Yet many other wealthy people who have arranged their finances to take advantage of loopholes and tax shelters will not

Chart 6.2

A Simple Tax Form for Business

Form 2 | **Business Tax** | **1999**

Business name	Employer identification number
Street address	County
City, town, or post office, state and ZIP code	Principal product

Line	Item	Line	Amount
1	Gross revenue from sales	1	
2	Allowable costs		
	(a) Purchases of goods, services, and materials	2(a)	
	(b) Wages, salaries, and retirement benefits	2(b)	
	(c) Purchases of capital equipment and land	2(c)	
3	Total allowable costs *(sum of lines 2(a), 2(b), and 2(c))*	3	
4	Taxable income *(line 1 less line 3)*	4	
5	Tax *(17% of line 4)*	5	
6	Carry-forward from 1998	6	
7	Interest on carry-forward *(6 percent of line 6)*	7	
8	Carry-forward into 1999 *(line 6 plus line 7)*	8	
9	Tax due *(line 5 less line 8, if positive)*	9	
10	Carry forward to 2000 *(line 8 less line 5, if positive)*	10	

Source: Office of Representative Richard Armey.

like losing these special privileges. And since a flat tax eliminates barriers to upward mobility, more people will climb the ladder of economic opportunity, which means wealth no longer will provide certain people with special status.

Businesses also will enjoy a greatly simplified system under the flat tax. Many of today's special loopholes will disappear, as will provisions in the code that make it hard for companies to invest, create jobs, and meet the challenge of international competition.

As the postcard included here illustrates, the business form is as simple as the individual form. All businesses are treated the same, and all business income is taxed, including interest and dividend income. Businesses simply would report total revenue from sales, subtract allowable costs (raw materials, wages, and capital expenditures), and pay a flat rate on the remainder.

Note that interest payments, dividend payments, and fringe benefits are not deductible. Thus, the business is responsible for withholding and paying tax on that income. To prevent bias against major investments, the business is allowed to carry forward unused tax deductions from previous years.

Some companies, particularly those that have relied on big lobbying staffs, will oppose such a flat tax. However, the majority of firms—particularly small and medium-sized businesses—will welcome a simple tax code that rewards them for doing well.

ENDING CLASS WARFARE

Even though the flat tax would force the wealthy to live by the same rules as everyone else, demagogues claim that it would allow the rich to keep too much of their money. Many of the arguments they make are demonstrably false or reflect an ignorance of history.

Consider, for instance, the charge that the flat tax will allow the rich to live tax-free from interest and dividends. This accusation stems from the fact that the individual postcard does not require taxpayers to report interest and dividend income. But taxes on that income *are* withheld and paid at the business level—a fact that helps to ensure that the rich will pay every penny they owe.

A more general assertion is that the flat tax is unfair because the rich will pay less in taxes. The reasoning behind this accusation is as follows: Currently, the rich face tax rates of around 40 percent, and much of their income is taxed more than once. Therefore, a flat tax means less tax revenue from the rich. This would be true if economic behavior did not change with changes in tax policy. In the real world, however, behavior *does* change. Because of an increased incentive to engage in productive behavior, it is certain that the rich will report more taxable income.

"The flat tax minimizes barriers to that climb, but in exchange requires that the rich play by the same rules as everyone else."

In fact, depending on how much more income they report—and the effect will be larger as time goes on—the wealthy could wind up paying a *greater* share of the tax burden under a flat tax. IRS data, for instance, show that the rich paid a greater share of the tax burden after the Reagan tax cuts than they had paid before the cuts. The same thing happened in the 1960s and the 1920s when tax rates were reduced.

People should not be singled out for punitive taxation simply because they have climbed the ladder of prosperity. Nor should they be allowed to manipulate the system and use high-priced lawyers, lobbyists, and accountants to avoid paying their fair share. High tax rates and double taxation simply encourage the rich to hide their money in tax shelters around the world.

This is precisely why the flat tax is the best way to tax everyone, especially the rich. People should be allowed to rise as far and as fast as their talents, abilities, and willingness to work will take them. The flat tax minimizes barriers to that climb, but in exchange requires that the rich play by the same rules as everyone else. As history demonstrates, this approach results in more tax revenue.

BENEFITS OF THE FLAT TAX

Although fairness and simplicity are important benefits of a flat tax, there are many others as well. A flat tax will lead to faster economic growth, higher wages, lower interest rates, and stronger communities. It will reduce political corruption by ending the sordid practice of trading campaign contributions for new deductions and tax shelters. Conversely, a flat tax also will stop politicians from engaging in social engineering and trying to micromanage the economy.

Simply put, the flat tax creates a level playing field that will unleash the entrepreneurial genius of the American people and allow our businesses to remain the best in the world. The only question is whether such a system is possible when so many special interests will fight to keep the current, loophole-ridden tax code. But this is a fight worth waging, because enacting a flat tax will:

- **Simplify the tax code.** Americans spend more than 5 billion hours each year trying to decipher 569 different tax forms. This paper chase costs the economy more than $150 billion annually in lost time, lawyers, accountants, and lobbyists.
- **Restore fairness.** A flat tax treats people equally. Rich people will pay their fair share, but the tax code no longer will penalize success and discriminate against citizens on the basis of income.
- **Reduce taxes.** The federal government is seizing more of our money than at any other point in our history, including

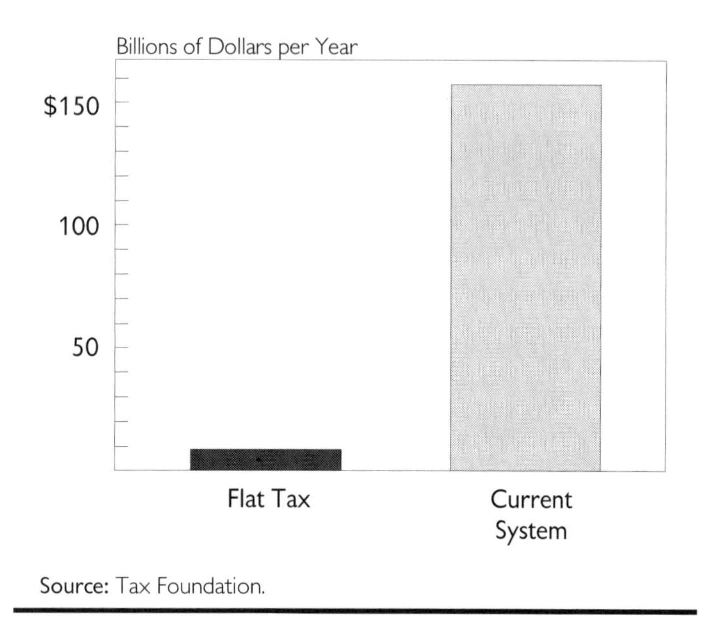

Source: Tax Foundation.

times of war. The average family now pays more in taxes than they pay for food, clothing, transportation, and housing combined. A low-rate flat tax, especially if the rate is set below 20 percent, will reduce this tax burden.

- **End political favoritism.** The flat tax will rid the code of all deductions, loopholes, credits, and special preferences. The only exemption will be a personal allowance based on family size. Politicians will lose the ability to pick winners and losers, reward friends and punish enemies, or use the tax code to impose their values on the economy.

- **Increase civil liberties.** Under current law, a taxpayer dealing with the Internal Revenue Service has fewer rights and protections than someone charged with murder. With a simple and fair flat tax, IRS infringements on freedoms and privacy will fall dramatically.
- **Protect the middle class.** Taxpayers often are punished with higher tax rates as they climb the economic ladder. Moving to a simple, single-rate tax system will let middle-class Americans keep more of their money and will facilitate upward mobility.
- **Produce faster economic growth.** By reducing tax penalties on productive economic behavior, a flat tax will spur work, savings, and investment. Even if long-term growth rose by as little as one-half of 1 percent (0.5 percent) per year, the annual income of an average family of four would be as much as $5,000 greater after ten years than it would be under current law.
- **Boost wealth.** According to Harvard economist Dale Jorgenson, the flat tax will boost national wealth by some $1 trillion. Because the flat tax will end the overtaxation of savings and investment, all income-producing assets will increase in value.
- **Generate more tax revenues from the wealthy.** The rich will pay more under a flat tax, but not because the tax code is confiscating more of their income and thereby encouraging tax shelters. Instead, the lower rates and prohibition against double taxation will increase their incentive to earn *and* report taxable income—which is precisely what happened in the 1920s, 1960s, and 1980s.

FEATURES OF THE FLAT TAX

The following list highlights some of the major features of the flat tax and briefly explains why they are essential to successful reform:

- **One tax rate.** Treating all taxpayers equally means not subjecting people to extra penalties when they contribute more to the nation's wealth. This is why tax rates should not rise as income increases. If you make ten times more than your neighbor, you should pay ten times more in taxes. And if Bill Gates makes 1,000 times more than you, he would pay 1,000 times more in taxes under a flat tax.

  Not only is this fair, but it also is sound economic policy. There is virtual unanimity among economists that low tax rates encourage greater economic activity than high tax rates. One rate also promotes simplicity and, just as important, makes it possible to tax capital income at the source.

  Finally, a single-rate tax system is less vulnerable to rate increases and other forms of political manipulation. Without a single rate, politicians would still be able to discriminate among income groups and constituents; it would be only a matter of time before the current tax code was re-created.

- **A generous family allowance.** The only exception to the rule about loopholes is that every taxpayer would be allowed to earn a decent income before the flat tax takes effect. A family of four, for instance, would not pay the tax on the first $30,000-plus of income.

- **Taxation of interest and dividends at the business level.** A single rate allows capital income (such as business income, dividends, and interest) to be taxed at the business level. This is important because it promotes simplicity and ensures that wealthy taxpayers cannot escape taxation.

  It is much easier to track and monitor one corporation or financial institution than it is to track and monitor millions of shareholders and depositors. It makes much more sense to have a company withhold and pay tax on profits than it does to make every shareholder pay taxes on his or her portion of the income. Likewise, having a bank withhold and pay taxes on interest income is preferable to asking the IRS to monitor everybody who has a bank account.

In effect, this is how wages and salaries are treated under the current system. Most employers withhold and pay income taxes to the government on behalf of their workers. The flat tax extends this system to other forms of income. Not only is this simple, but it also ensures that the rich—who receive larger amounts of interest and dividend income—have no way to avoid taxes. Simply stated, the income is taxed before it reaches their pockets.

- **No double taxation of savings.** The current tax code makes consumption more attractive than savings. How? Once income is earned and taxes are paid, workers have two choices about how to use the money that is left. They can consume it, in which case the benefits of consumption are not taxed. Or they can save the money, in which case the benefits of savings—such as interest, dividends, and capital gains—are subject to tax. This double taxation of income that is saved and invested is particularly foolish; every economic theory—even Marxism—acknowledges that capital formation (savings and investment) is the key to long-term growth and rising wages.

  Since the bias against savings in the current code is caused by taxing income when it is earned and then taxing the returns on any income that is saved, it can be solved by eliminating one of these two layers of tax. This can be done by creating either a traditional individual retirement account (IRA) or a back-ended (or Roth) IRA. In either case, taxpayers would be subject to no restrictions on how much income they could place in their savings account.

  With a traditional IRA, tax on all money deposited would be deferred, but taxes would be levied on both principal and interest when the money is withdrawn. With back-ended IRAs, investors pay a tax on all their income right away, but they do not have to pay a second layer of tax on subsequent earnings. In either case, the income is taxed only one time, and either approach is acceptable.

The flat tax uses the back-ended IRA approach (except for pensions, which would receive traditional IRA treatment). This approach is simpler to administer because the government does not need to track accounts. It also promotes privacy because taxpayers do not have to let the government know about their assets.

- **No capital gains tax.** Only income is taxed under a flat tax, not changes in net worth. And since the capital gains tax is nothing but a tax on an asset that increased in value, it would be repealed under a flat tax. Capital gains taxes are another form of double taxation. Taxing any increase in the value of an asset purchased with after-tax dollars is simply a second layer of tax.

  Another way to understand the proper tax treatment of capital gains is to remember why assets rise in value. A stock rises in value because of the market's expectation of an increase in the future stream of income that it will produce. That income should be taxed when and if it actually is earned. To tax the expectation as well as the actual income is double taxation.

- **No death tax.** The estate tax is a tax on the transfer of assets upon death. Since an estate is the accumulation of after-tax income that is saved or invested, any subsequent layer of taxation is double taxation and further biases the tax code in favor of consumption.

- **No tax on Social Security benefits.** Under the flat tax, there is no deduction for money that is paid to Social Security. In effect, this means that workers pay income tax on their payroll taxes. Because there should not be another layer of taxation when those same workers receive retirement benefits from Social Security, the flat tax leaves benefits untouched.

In other words, even though Social Security is a government entitlement program that transfers money from workers to retirees, it will be treated like real savings under the flat tax. This arrangement also will be ideal if Social Security is reformed in a way that allows workers to have private retirement accounts.

- **No itemized deductions.** Although deductions receive the most attention in tax reform debates, the importance of itemized deductions is vastly overblown. Retaining the major deductions under a flat tax would add some complexity to the code and violate the principle that all taxpayers should be treated equally, but the impact would be minor.

  Nevertheless, there is no reason to make such a concession. Support for the flat tax is driven by the public's desire for fairness and simplicity. If the loss of itemized deductions causes anxiety in taxpayers, that concern is a proxy for their fear that tax reform will mean paying more in taxes. If their tax bill falls, most such concerns will vanish.

  Moreover, as other chapters in this book explain, there is no reason to believe that a flat tax will have any adverse impact on housing or charities. Briefly stated, a thriving economy is the best guarantee of home ownership and charitable giving.

- **No alternative minimum tax.** Individuals and businesses often are subject to the alternative minimum tax (AMT), a quirky provision that forces taxpayers to calculate their taxes using two different methods and then pay the government the higher of the two amounts. Because the AMT is likely to take effect when deductions are "too large" relative to income, it is likely to affect a business most during hard times. Under a flat tax, however, every individual and business is treated the same. This eliminates the need for an AMT to catch taxpayers who supposedly are not paying enough.

- **Expensing instead of depreciation.** Under current law, businesses are not allowed to deduct fully the cost of investments. Under a fair and neutral tax code, taxable profits should equal total revenue minus total costs, including any money spent to purchase machinery, equipment, and land. The flat tax achieves this goal by permitting all enterprises to expense all capital purchases immediately in the first year.

CONCLUSION

The flat tax is not the only good tax reform proposal being discussed today. The national sales tax, which David Burton of the Argus Group discusses in another chapter, also would treat all taxpayers equally and increase prosperity.

Ultimately, what matters most is that the current tax code is abolished and replaced by a fair and simple tax system. The longer Americans are burdened with an abusive IRS and today's convoluted tax code, the harder it will be for our nation to maintain its number-one economic status. Repealing the current system and passing a flat tax will ensure that our children and grandchildren enjoy even greater levels of prosperity than we enjoy today.

Randy Tate, Executive Director of the Christian Coalition, has led the Coalition's grassroots efforts and lobbying activities on Capitol Hill since June 1997 to ensure that legislation passed by Congress strengthens the American family. One of the issues the Coalition worked on during the most recent session of Congress, for example, was elimination of the marriage tax penalty. In 1988, at the age of 22, Mr. Tate became the second youngest person ever elected to the Washington state legislature; he served three terms in the State House of Representatives and rose to the position of Republican Caucus Chairman. In 1994, he was elected to the U.S. House of Representatives for Washington's Ninth Congressional District. Mr. Tate received his B.A. in economics and political science from Western Washington University.

7

HELPING THE MIDDLE CLASS

Randy Tate
Executive Director, Christian Coalition

When the people of Israel decided to reject God's rule and install one of their own men as king, God instructed the prophet Samuel to warn them of the "procedure of the king who will reign over them." The Old Testament tells us that Samuel cautioned that a king will impose taxes on the people, exacting a tenth of their income and possessions. While the Israelites thus far had been obligated only to contribute a tenth of their income and possessions to the Lord in the form of a tithe, their King Saul would now demand the same portion for himself as well.

If only the prophet Samuel could have given the same warning to Members of Congress in 1913, the year the federal income tax was enacted. Incredibly modest by today's standards, that tax applied only to the wealthiest two-fifths of 1 percent, and the top tax rate was only 7 percent. Proponents of this tax promised that the top rate could never conceivably top 10 percent. Like their counterparts in Samuel's day, they did not understand the enticing nature of the power to tax.

Then, as now, government had a difficult time keeping its promises and restraining its appetites. The slippery slope soon turned into a tidal wave, and within a few short years—spurred by two world wars and the Great Depression—government was taxing more and more families at higher and higher rates.

Chart 7.1

Taxes Take Biggest Share of Family Budget

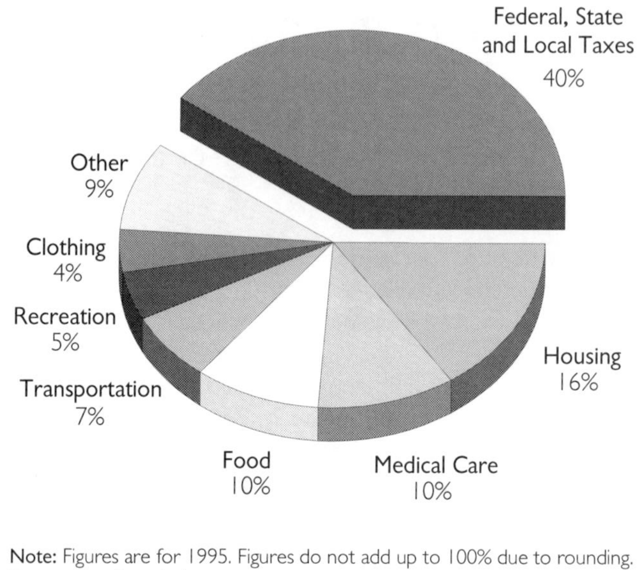

Note: Figures are for 1995. Figures do not add up to 100% due to rounding.
Source: Tax Foundation.

Today, the average family now pays more in taxes than it pays for food, clothing, housing, and transportation combined.

Average Workers Bear the Cost. Much of this increase is due to the rapid expansion of the federal government. Before the income tax, Washington played a very small role in our lives. Politicians respected the Constitution's limits on federal power. But the creation of an income tax proved too tempting, and the biggest victims have been the middle class.

Consider, for instance, the impact of the federal income tax and the payroll tax. In 1948, these taxes took only about 3 percent of an average family's income. Today, they confiscate nearly a fourth of the family budget. Add corporate taxes, excise taxes, import taxes, state taxes, and local taxes, and it is little wonder that so many families have to send both parents into the work force.

If lawmakers in 1913 had had any idea of the monster they were creating, all but the most defiantly socialist Members of Congress no doubt would have rejected it resoundingly. Yet who could have dared to imagine that a system designed initially to tax the Rockefellers would become the grotesque, bewilderingly complex federal tax code we have today, confiscating such a big share of the average family's income?

What makes this so painful is that our nation has survived, indeed prospered, for most of its existence without an income tax or an Internal Revenue Service. Indeed, an income tax was regarded as so contrary to American ideals that when Congress in 1894 tried to pass a mere 2 percent income tax on the superwealthy, the Supreme Court struck it down as unconstitutional. Only after amending the U.S. Constitution in 1913 could Congress impose an income tax—and the rest, as they say, is tragic history. Americans who would "render unto Caesar the things that are Caesar's, and unto God the things that are God's" are finding Uncle Sam to be an increasingly avaricious Caesar.

Restoring Sound Values. We know what the problem is, but what should be done? Philosopher Michael Novak has an acute grasp of the moral dimensions of economic policy. He describes the three pillars necessary for a free and virtuous society: political liberty, economic liberty, and cultural liberty. All three are interdependent, and to undermine any one of the pillars places the foundation of society itself in grave danger. More than any other nation in history, America has enshrined and protected these principles, prompting British historian Paul Johnson to describe the American experiment in ordered liberty as "the first, best hope for the human race."

Tax policy is merely one component of a strong and virtuous society. Vibrant democracy, individual liberties, healthy families, robust religious institutions, and the rule of law all contribute necessarily to a strong America. To the extent that our current tax system violates basic principles of fairness, efficiency, and liberty, it also undercuts rather than reinforces those other values and institutions that sustain our nation.

In 1997, Congress enacted the first tax cut in 16 years. Although this was a small victory, such measures are like giving a car an oil change when its engine is failing: It may improve performance for a while, but it fails to fix the root problem. Our current tax code is terminally ill. Fundamental, radical reform is needed—not just cosmetic tinkering around the edges and under the hood. Despite the diversity of opinion in America today on just about every subject imaginable, virtually all Americans would agree that the current income tax system must go. And the IRS should go with it.

Tax reform, above all, must promote the interests of the middle class. The persistence of a robust middle class is one of the unique characteristics of American society. Fully 80 percent of Americans consider themselves middle-class, and proudly so. The middle class has been an anchor of unity and stability throughout American history, resisting the stratification and divisions that have proven so destructive in other societies. The vast middle class bridges many other gaps in America society—be they ethnic, religious, financial, or political. It defines American values and opportunity.

We need a tax code that matches those values. How, then, should we begin the process of reforming and replacing our anti-family, anti-growth, anti-prosperity tax code?

THE FLAT TAX

I believe we should implement a simple, fair system that taxes income only one time and at one low rate—in short, a flat tax.

Much of the rhetoric against the flat tax dismisses it as a gimmick for the rich, but the reality is that it could be the best news for hard-working American families since the microwave oven and the minivan.

One concern about the flat tax is whether the middle class would benefit. We know that the flat tax repeals destructively high tax rates and eliminates double taxation of savings. This will be good for the rich (at least those who are not upset because they lose their tax shelters). But the flat tax is also great news for the poor and working poor because of the big family allowance (more on this later). Indeed, many lower-income taxpayers will be off the income tax rolls altogether.

So if the rich come out ahead and the poor escape the tax completely, are middle-class families left paying the bills? Back when we had a big budget deficit, this was a serious concern. After all, if the new tax system had to raise just as much money as the current tax code, where else would the money be found?

This, however, is no longer an issue. America today is enjoying a remarkable economic boom that began with the Reagan tax cuts and has continued, with one small interruption, ever since. In recent years, this growth has been sustained, at least in part, by a balanced budget, tax cuts, welfare reform, and other responsible policies advocated and implemented by Congress (and embraced, belatedly, by Bill Clinton).

As supply-siders have always told us, a healthy economy causes tax revenues to rise. With more people working, family incomes climbing, and business profits growing, government coffers are overflowing. As a result, federal budget forecasters are predicting a tremendous federal budget surplus over the next ten years—perhaps as much as $2.7 trillion.

Remember, that is your money. But as experience and the very nature of government have taught us only too well, the federal government will look for any possible way to spend that money. The only way to stop it is to give the money back to the people, and here is where we can make a virtue out of necessity. We know that we need to cut taxes. We also know that it is important to fix the tax code. Finally, we know that the middle class deserves a break.

> *"Much of the rhetoric against the flat tax dismisses it as a gimmick for the rich, but the reality is that it could be the best news for hard-working American families since the microwave oven and the minivan."*

The answer is to combine tax reform with a big tax cut. This accomplishes two goals. First, Washington bureaucrats and special interests will not be able to spend the "surplus" (a clever word for excessive taxation) on big government programs. Just as important, thanks to all this extra money, we can enact a flat tax with a low rate; and if the rate can be set below 20 percent, the vast majority of taxpayers will enjoy lower tax bills.

In other words, never has there been a more opportune time to redesign our tax system. Americans agree that a new approach is needed, and a productive economy and improvements in fiscal policy have given us the financial resources to implement bold new plans.

The skeptic might object, arguing that the overall prosperity of the U.S. economy today demonstrates that we do not need major tax reform. I could not disagree more. First of all, we do not know what the future will hold. If we want growth to remain strong, and if we want to avoid the economic turmoil affecting the rest of the world, tax reform and tax cuts are a good insurance policy.

More important, however, I do not measure economic growth and prosperity only in terms of gross domestic product (GDP), the Dow Jones average, and per capita income. I measure it in terms of the quality of life among average, hard-working American families: Do both parents have to hold down full-time jobs merely to make ends meet? Are they able to take time off for family vacations? Are they free to arrive home at a decent hour for family dinner, or make time for their children's soccer games and school plays? Can they set aside enough money to pay the increasingly expensive but increasingly necessary costs of college? Are they able to give generously to their churches, synagogues, and meaningful charities? Do they suffer constant stress and pressure from lack of financial security?

In short, tax policies are not helping American families achieve financial security. This is why real reform is needed.

PRO-FAMILY TAX REFORM

The flat tax will amount to a considerable tax cut for the vast majority of American families; it will increase wages and economic growth; and it will distribute the benefits of that growth equitably across America. Perhaps most appealingly, it will render impotent the tyrannical bureaucrats at the IRS and close the loopholes and hidden benefits that too many special interests have built into the current Pandora's box known as the federal tax code.

> *"Just as important, thanks to all this extra money, we can enact a flat tax with a low rate; and if the rate can be set below 20 percent, the vast majority of taxpayers will enjoy lower tax bills."*

Without delving into the mind-numbing minutiae of charts, figures, and statistics, I believe it will be helpful to take a simple, commonsense look at some of the basic features of a single-rate tax and explain why it will benefit America's middle-class families.

A flat tax would provide a much-needed tax break to American families. The average family struggles perpetually against a stifling tax burden. You would be hard-pressed to find any

American family today who thinks they don't pay enough and ought to pay more in taxes! And the tax burden seems to grow and grow. Since 1955, 52 percent of the growth in wages for the typical single-earner family has been sent to the government, and a staggering 59 percent of the growth in wages for two-earner families has gone to pay higher taxes.

In 1998, Americans had to work until May 10 to satisfy the demands of federal, state, and local tax collectors. Throw in government regulations, and they work until June 25—almost half of the entire year—just to pay the cost of government. This is not right. Medieval serfs had to give the Lord of the Manor only one-third of their output. American families deserve better.

The benefits of a flat tax will be felt directly by American families. The current tax code permits a family of four to shield about $18,000 from taxation. Although I am not endorsing any specific flat tax proposal, just about any flat tax would enable that same family of four to protect almost twice as much income (from $33,000 to $36,000) from the greedy hands of the federal government. This is why families making $15,000 to $35,000 a year will benefit most from the big tax cut offered by a flat tax. We all must do our part to help the poor, and I cannot think of a better start than exempting them completely from federal income taxes.

Equal Treatment. Some have objected that the flat tax treats the rich, the middle class, and the poor alike—but that is precisely the point. Unlike our present tax code, which attempts to impose higher marginal rates on people who earn more, a flat tax system is non-discriminatory and fundamentally fair. Of course, many other taxes are based on a single rate, such as the sales tax. No one is arguing that the rich ought to pay a 12 percent sales tax, the middle class 8 percent, and the poor 4 percent when they buy the same television. All should pay the same rate.

Chart 7.2

The Rich Paid a Greater Share of Income Tax Burden After Reagan Tax Cuts

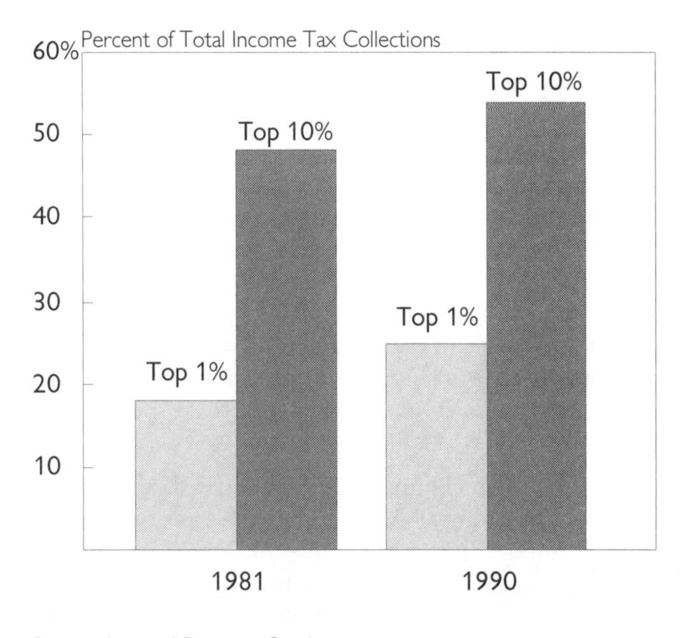

Source: Internal Revenue Service.

Although, as Chart 7.2 shows, the rich have paid more of the income tax burden since Reagan's tax cuts, under a flat tax system, the rich will pay more—much more—in taxes than the poor. The "flat" in "flat tax" does not refer to a single amount, only to a single rate. Unfair would be requiring all Americans to pay, say, $1,000 each year in taxes regardless of income.

The key to the essential fairness of the flat tax lies in the fact that by taxing people at the same equal rate, it will require those with more income to pay a higher amount. The rich, the poor, the middle class, and everyone else will pay their "fair share." The flat tax is fair precisely because the rich, who earn much more, will pay much more than the poor. The fabulously wealthy movie star or professional athlete who makes one million times as much money as the local plumber will pay one million times as much in taxes.

Eliminating Tax Shelters. The hidden irony in the current tax system is that while it purports to impose higher tax rates on those who earn more, to the point where the top marginal rate stands at an onerous 40 percent, it also contains thousands of loopholes and special tax breaks. Many of the wealthiest individuals and special interests have become quite adept at avoiding the 40 percent income tax rate by hiring lobbyists and tax lawyers to take advantage of favorable loopholes—loopholes that are not available to the average taxpayer. Sometimes, they pay no income tax at all. Critics who dismiss the flat tax as a "tax cut just for the rich" blithely disregard these special-interest loopholes.

Closing loopholes, eliminating special-interest tax breaks and deductions, and taxing all Americans at the same rate has a twofold advantage. It does not punish hard-working Americans by imposing higher tax rates just for being productive and successful. And it does not allow privileged special interests to manipulate the tax code for their own benefit and thereby escape paying their fair share. A flat tax system restores equality to its rightful place among the cardinal American virtues.

More Prosperity. The benefits of a flat tax system only begin with its fairness. It also will spur our economy to even more dynamic, widespread growth—growth that benefits all American families. The flat tax will increase wages and make it easier to support a family on just one income.

A government that defends "family values" has to have a tax system that values families. Yet American families who work hard and want to save or invest suffer greatly under the current tax system. First, their earnings are taxed, and then any profits they make on their savings and investments are taxed again. All of the talk in Washington about the need to save and pay off the national debt shamefully disregards the fact that our tax system punishes families who try to save and stay out of debt themselves.

By taxing income only once, a flat tax system would reward rather than discourage savings and investment. Small family businesses will have incentives to invest on the basis of what makes the most financial sense, not the best tax write-off. This, in turn, will stimulate productivity, higher wages, and better economic health for American families. Businesses will earn more, employers will pay more, and families will keep more of their money.

Note that the emphasis is on families. Not only will they be able to save more for family trips and their children's education, but they will be able to pass on more assets from one generation to the next.

An additional benefit of a single-rate tax is that it will eliminate the insidious "marriage penalty." This is the ridiculous provision whereby married couples bear a heavier tax burden than a man and woman who live together and file as individuals. The family allowance in a flat tax would provide a married couple twice as much protection as that afforded a single taxpayer.

Simplicity. Perhaps the most immediate, tangible appeal of the flat tax is its simplicity. As any American who has had to wade through today's tax forms knows, the current system of mounting paperwork and frustration cannot continue. The system's complexity and density boggle even the experts.

The IRS sends out 8 billion pages of forms and instructions every year—enough to circle the earth 28 times if laid end to end. A study commissioned by the IRS itself estimates that Americans each year devote 5.4 billion hours to complying with the tax code at an annual cost of anywhere from $159 billion to $232 billion. Worst of all, all this time and money offers no guarantee of a right answer. No wonder a public opinion poll found that taxpayers would rather undergo a root canal than an IRS audit.

Given that the current system contains staggering hidden costs in money and time, and also engenders genuine misery among taxpayers, it is no wonder that people demand a change. A flat tax, almost breathtaking in its simplicity, consists of a mere postcard and can be filled out in minutes by just about anyone. Elementary school children could do the family taxes as a homework assignment.

To paraphrase a popular credit card commercial, while a single-rate tax would save 5.4 billion labor hours and around $200 billion in compliance costs, what it saves in peace of mind is priceless. Such a system might change the career objectives of a few accountants, tax lawyers, and IRS agents, but it would put the rest of America back in business.

One objection frequently raised about a single-rate tax system is that some current proposals would curtail popular tax deductions like charitable gifts. In the interest of strengthening our churches and civil society, I have a strong interest in a tax system that reinforces these values. I do believe policymakers should think long and hard about this issue.

Elaine Chao makes a compelling case elsewhere in this book that charitable contributions would increase under a pure flat tax, but this is not just about dollars and cents. It is also about the message government is sending. Private, voluntary institutions, not government spending programs, are needed to help the less fortunate. Therefore, I believe a single-rate tax system can—and should—preserve charitable deductions.

Freedom. At the end of the day, the question of tax reform and a single-rate tax system is about much more than paperwork, tax savings, deductions, and offsetting costs. It is about the values we hold as Americans and the principles that define not just how we earn and spend our money, but how we organize our society and live our lives.

Our ancestors, especially our grandparents and parents, bequeathed a precious heritage to us. American freedom has been secured through generations of tremendous sacrifice. We must remain vigilant in protecting these priceless liberties both from large tyrannies abroad and small encroachments at home.

Cynics and liberals say the flat tax appeals to greed, but the real greed is among those who believe the federal government has the right to confiscate money from America's families. They also would have us believe that we should be thankful if government allows us to keep any of what we earn.

I operate from a different presumption. The money that America's families work hard to earn is theirs by right, and it is only through the consent of the people that governments are authorized to collect taxes fairly, efficiently, and responsibly. That is not greed; it is freedom.

Michael Farris, an author, ordained minister, constitutional lawyer, and father of ten, is one of the leading pro-family activists on Capitol Hill. He has argued cases in courts across the nation, including before the United States Supreme Court, five U.S. circuit courts of appeal, seven state supreme courts, and five state courts of appeal. Mr. Farris is founder and president of the Home School Legal Defense Association. His daily radio show, "Home School Heartbeat," is heard on over 700 stations. He has written eight books, including a high school textbook on constitutional law and two books on fathering. Ordained in 1983, Mr. Farris currently serves as interim pastor for the Blue Ridge Bible Church. He received his J.D. degree with honors from Gonzaga University School of Law, where he also served as Articles Editor of the Law Review.

8

FIXING THE TAX CODE'S ANTI-FAMILY BIAS

Michael Farris
President, Home School Legal Defense Association

There are some "family issues" of such transcendent moral import that pro-family advocates rightly give them priority. But few issues considered on Capitol Hill affect the day-to-day lives of every family in America nearly as much as the federal income tax. Although some level of taxation is inevitable, our tax system has become a confiscatory "crazy quilt" that contains significant penalties against both married couples and large families.

This is wrong. It is bad social policy. It is bad economic policy. It is bad family policy. The time has come to repeal the tax code and start over. Only fundamental reform will allow us to clean out the Augean stables of special-interest complexity. A simple and fair system like the flat tax will give families the freedom to live their lives without being punished or manipulated by Washington.

The Marriage Penalty. The marriage penalty is a well-known feature of the Internal Revenue Code. According to a June 1997 report by the Congressional Budget Office (CBO), nearly 21 million American couples are victims of the marriage penalty, which costs them, on average, an extra $1,400 in income tax each year.

What is not well-known is that a marriage penalty is essentially inherent in a system with graduated income tax rates. The CBO acknowledges that this is the case, writing in its report that "A tax structure with progressive rates, however, cannot attain both goals [marriage neutrality and equal treatment]." Politicians in Washington apparently believe that income redistribution is more important than equal treatment for married couples.

According to the Internal Revenue Service (IRS), the first $42,350 of a married couple's 1998 income is taxed at 15 percent. Above that level, their income is taxed at 28 percent. Yet two unmarried wage earners who live together can earn a combined $50,700 before being bumped into the higher tax bracket. As a result, the couple living together can save more than $1,000 on that extra $8,350 of income.

This is wrong. When unmarried couples earn more and are taxed at a lower rate than a married couple earning a comparable amount, then the tax code has imposed a financial penalty on marriage.

The Large Family Penalty. Another anti-family penalty built into the tax code, though not nearly as well-known as the marriage penalty, is the large family penalty. The current tax code strips away personal exemptions, itemized deductions, and (starting with 1998 returns) the $400-per-child tax credit as income rises. This causes punitive tax rates for workers, small business owners, and entrepreneurs who are climbing the economic ladder.

For example, consider four married couples, each with an adjusted gross income of $202,500. As Table 5.1 shows, families with more children pay higher marginal tax rates—even though there is less income per family member.

Defenders of the current tax code argue that it is predicated on the notion of fairness—meaning that the tax falls most heavily on those with the greatest ability to pay. As the father of

Table 8.1

The Large Family Tax Penalty

	Family Size			
	No Children	2 Children	4 Children	10 Children
Marginal Tax Rate	37.9%	39.4%	40.9%	45.5%
Additional Tax on Last $2,500 in Earnings	$948	$986	$1,024	$1,139
Per Capita Income	$101,250	$50,625	$33,750	$16,875

Note: The marginal tax rate is the rate on the last $2,500 of an adjusted gross income of $202,500. The example assumes $50,000 in itemized deductions for each family. It excludes consideration of the $400 per child tax credit.

ten children, I strongly dispute the contention that the tax code is fair to large families. A family the size of mine pays almost $200 more in tax for every $2,500 in additional earnings than is paid by a two-income family with no children.

Let's look at it from another perspective. Is it fair that a tax system imposes a marginal tax rate of 37.9 percent on a family with a per capita income of $101,250 and a 45.5 percent tax rate on a family with a per capita income of $16,875? I would not complain if my family paid the same marginal tax rate as one comprised of two childless wage earners. But to charge me a higher marginal rate is, frankly, infuriating.

"Is it fair that a tax system imposes a marginal tax rate of 37.9 percent on a family with a per capita income of $101,250 and a 45.5 percent tax rate on a family with a per capita income of $16,875?"

I have found the state income tax system in Virginia to be far flatter and much fairer to families. There are no phase-outs of deductions or personal exemptions; thus, the marginal tax rate is the same on small and large families alike. Although there are four tax rates in Virginia, the differences are minimal. The first $3,000 in income is taxed at 2 percent. The next $2,000 is taxed at 3 percent. From $5,001 to $17,000, the tax is 5 percent. All income over $17,000 is taxed at 5.75 percent. Nearly 90 percent of all taxpayers (86.9 percent) are in either the 5 percent or the 5.75 percent bracket.

In terms of overall fairness, Virginia's "almost flat" tax clearly places the greatest burden on taxpayers with the highest incomes. According to the 1996 Governor's Tax Commission, Virginia taxpayers with incomes over $100,000 file only 4.9 percent of all tax returns, but this small segment of the population pays 25.6 percent of all personal income taxes. The second highest group, with incomes from $75,000 to $99,999, comprises 5 percent of the population and pays 11.9 percent of all state income taxes. Together, the highest earners comprise 10 percent of Virginia's tax filers, but they pay 37.5 percent of the total taxes received. A flat tax at the national level would have the same effect.

FAMILIES NEED TAX CUTS, NOT TAX GIMMICKS

The Internal Revenue Code is a nightmare. Over the years, Congress has responded to shrill voices and fulfilled the requests of lobbyists and campaign contributors who asked for special favors. There is some temptation to organize pro-family forces to get our own special arrangements. Yet this is a zero-sum game, one that special interests are much more adept at playing.

With the system the way it is now, however, what choice is there? Home schooling families tend to have large numbers of children. We could argue in favor of repealing the penalty on

Chart 8.1

Tax Deductions Offer Little Relief to the Poor and Middle Class

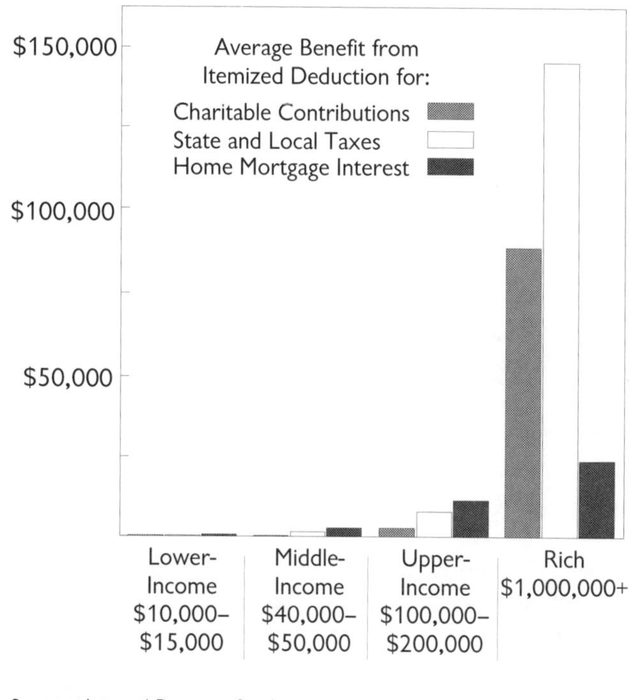

Source: Internal Revenue Service.

large families in the current code. Like many other middle-class taxpayers, many home schooling families have been hit hard by the alternative minimum tax (AMT). This is the bizarre provision that forces taxpayers to figure out their taxes two ways and pay the IRS whichever amount is higher. Talk about adding insult to injury! We could seek repeal of this crazy provision.

These changes would be welcome, and consistent with a flat tax, but even a successful campaign to fix the AMT would fail to cure the Internal Revenue Code's two central problems: (1) it is riddled with unfair gimmicks and exceptions, and (2) the total taxes families pay are simply too high. Family advocates need to work to replace the entire tax code. It is impossible to fix the current system—a monstrosity that resembles something my children might construct out of Legos, wooden blocks, soda cans, and extra body parts from old Barbie dolls.

Tax Freedom Day

1902	January 31
1913	January 30
1925	February 6
1930	February 13
1940	March 8
1950	March 24
1960	April 16
1970	April 26
1980	May 1
1984	April 28
1988	May 2
1992	April 30
1996	May 7
1997	May 9
1998	May 10

It is bad enough that the tax code is riddled with unfair provisions that result in numerous inequities, but the rate of taxation continues to grow to the point where Americans have become servants of the government in a manner that is unacceptable in a free society. The Tax Foundation reports that the average American family worked until May 10, 1998, before earning enough to pay all federal, state, and local taxes. This date, known as Tax Freedom Day, has been getting deeper and deeper into the year, following a trend that began shortly after the income tax was enacted in 1913. Only during the Reagan years was there some movement of Tax Freedom Day in the right direction.

As the box shows, President Clinton's 1993 tax increase had an effect, but not one that is good for families. The average American worked more than one week longer for government in 1998 than in 1992. It is highly doubtful that this is the kind of government taxation our forefathers had in mind when they penned in the Preamble to the Constitution that they were creating this government "to secure the Blessings of Liberty to ourselves and our Posterity." Unfortunately, their posterity is "blessed" only with a mammoth government that has developed an insatiable appetite for taxes.

THE FLAT TAX, PRO-FAMILY SOLUTION

A flat income tax, with a generous exemption based on family size, is the best solution for lowering taxes and promoting the fundamental fairness that American families deserve. According to research by the prestigious Tax Foundation, the flat tax bill introduced in the 105th Congress by House Majority Leader Richard Armey (R–TX) and Senator Richard Shelby (R–AL) would benefit all income groups in terms of overall tax savings. The difference between the taxes that would be paid by four "typical" families under the current system and what would be paid by the same four families under a 17 percent and 20 percent flat tax as contemplated by the Armey–Shelby plan is shown in Table 5.2.

Under a flat tax plan, all deductions, exemptions, exceptions, and special favors would be eliminated—save one. There would be a generous family income exemption for a single person or a married couple. In addition, there would be another generous personal exemption for each dependent.

Under the flat tax, a family of four would earn up to $33,000 tax-free. This is a sizable increase over the current allowance of $18,000 for this same family of four. For those who have families of other sizes, the per-child exemption under this flat tax plan would be $5,000. Thus, a family with five children could earn $38,000 tax-free, and families with ten children could earn

Table 8.2

How Much Would a Typical Family Save in Taxes Under a Flat Tax?

Annual Earnings	Current Tax	17% Flat Tax	20% Flat Tax	Tax Savings 17%/20%
$25,000	$32	0	0	$32/$32
$50,000	$4,271	$2,819	$3,316	$1,452/$955
$75,000	$8,159	$6,822	$8,026	$1,337/$133
$100,000	$13,113	$10,106	$11,889	$3,007/$1,224

Note: All families are assumed to have two children and have the national average in itemized deductions.

$63,000 before Uncle Sam joins them at the kitchen table—heaven knows they need every penny.

It is true that the nearly sacred mortgage and charitable giving itemized deductions would be eliminated by a flat tax. As a church elder and long-time head of a nonprofit organization, however, it seems obvious to me that churches and charities would be far better off in the long run under a flat tax. The threat that the IRS might remove a group's tax-exempt status has turned many a leader into a coward. But removing the exemption will not hurt the groups that are doing good work; they will prosper. Those whose only justification for existence is the deductibility of a gift perhaps deserve to falter.

As for the mortgage deduction, there is something fundamentally unfair in the notion that those who are paying for their homes should deduct their interest expenses from their tax bill while those who rent, or those who diligently paid off their mortgages, should get no such break. The unfairness of the current system is multiplied by the fact that people who own homes can take out second mortgages for pleasure items, college expenses, or travel and get to deduct interest payments. Those who rent cannot deduct the costs of their boats, education, or vacations.

The system unfairly rewards homeowners and promotes dangerous levels of debt. People should be encouraged to live debt-free, not to be subsidized if they incur certain kinds of favored debts. The flat tax not only would create a level playing field for all housing expenses, but also would eliminate the homeowner-gets-to-deduct-his-ski-boat gimmickry in the current system.

Simplicity and Growth. Both the marriage penalty and the large family penalty would disappear under a flat tax. The marriage penalty would be erased with the elimination of graduated tax brackets. After a family has earned the tax-free income permitted by the personal and dependent exemptions, all additional income is taxed at a single flat rate. Single taxpayers get a personal exemption that is exactly one-half of the exemption for married couples. There is no penalty for marriage or remaining single. And since the various "phase-outs" in the current code are eliminated, the egregious large family penalty will be eliminated by the flat tax.

The truly important thing to understand is the inherent superiority of a tax system that imposes only one rate and allows only one form of exemption—a basic per-person earnings exemption. Graduated tax rates provide a huge disincentive to work hard. The more a person earns, the steeper the penalty that is imposed on the added earnings. Such a system also provides huge incentives to hide income. Some people hide income by simply cheating. Others effectively hide income by successfully lobbying Congress to give them gimmicky tax breaks, such as the infamous oil depletion allowance that gave a break to people who owned oil wells.

The complexity of the current system is indicated by the 569 forms that are in use for individuals and businesses, not only to comply with the tax law, but also to take advantage of all the special rules that Congress has created to reward various constituencies over the years. The complexity of the code is one of the best indicators of its unfairness. For every special tax avoidance rule (such as allowing homeowners to deduct the interest on a ski boat purchase if they finance it through a second mortgage), there is a parallel inequity (non-homeowners cannot deduct the interest on their ski boat purchases).

All such special rules have the tendency to encourage certain kinds of behavior and discourage others. The tax code intrudes into the autonomy of the family by placing artificial incentives to make decisions that are favored by the government. Families, not government, should decide what is best for them. A flat tax does not reward one behavior or punish another. All financial decisions made by families are treated with absolute, evenhanded neutrality.

An important additional benefit of a flat tax is the virtual elimination of compliance costs. Gone will be the days when an expensive trip to a tax preparer or accountant is necessary around April 15. Tax returns can be prepared in 15 minutes or less for every family, and an individual income tax return can fit on a postcard (which should be mailed inside an envelope for privacy reasons). The simple steps in filling it out include: How much did you make? How many people are in your family? Deduct the family allowance. Multiply what is left by the single, low tax rate. Write in the amount due. Mail the postcard (with a check if needed).

> *"The tax code intrudes into the autonomy of the family by placing artificial incentives to make decisions that are favored by the government."*

Families with small businesses (or large businesses, for that matter) also will find that the flat tax drastically reduces the

Chart 8.2

The Economy Is Not a Fixed Pie: Sound Economic Policy Benefits All Income Groups

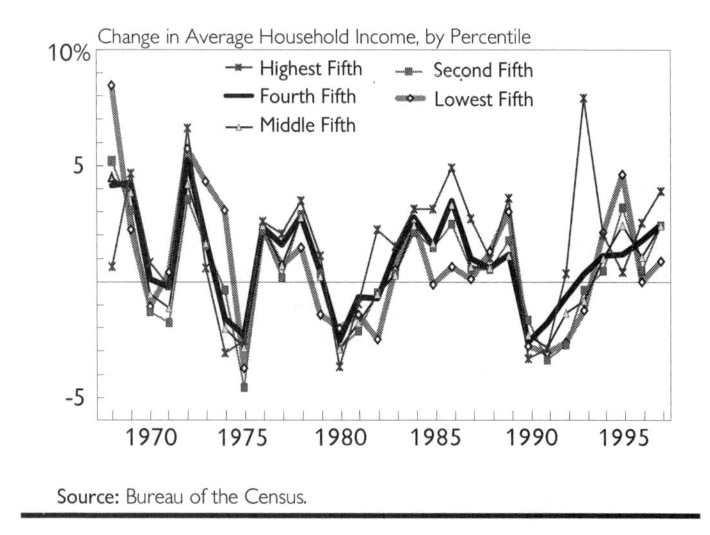

Source: Bureau of the Census.

paperwork required for tax compliance. Businesses will welcome the fact that the tax code now rewards companies that do well in the marketplace rather than those which play the Washington game (unless the business is one that benefits from the favored tax avoidance rules). Business returns also would fit on a single postcard, and dividends and interest would be taxed only once, not twice as they are under the current tax system.

The family is not only the basic social unit of American society, but also the basic economic unit. Economic growth—at least economic growth that results from even-handed rules that diminish the role of government—inherently advances the economic well-being of families. When a father has a job, the family is helped. If Mom wants to stay home, and the combination of tax cuts and increased opportunities for Dad makes that possible, the family is helped. The flat tax will help families by launching the most pro-growth economic approach in the past century.

A recent trip to Mexico demonstrated to me the value that strong economic growth brings to average families. People who go to work for large American companies in Mexico are lifted out of poverty and brought into a growing Mexican middle class. The standard of living rises for every family when there are better job opportunities available.

We need to make it financially viable for American companies to expand opportunities to lift workers to the next rung in the economic ladder at home as well. Bad domestic economic policies lead to the exportation of jobs and the loss of opportunities for American breadwinners. Good tax policy will help to keep American jobs in America.

Home schooling families (to choose a group familiar to me) have a great deal of interest in starting home-based businesses, either to supplement income or eventually to become the primary source of income. The flat tax makes such businesses more realistic by lowering tax compliance costs, and makes the rewards for hard work more productive by lowering tax rates.

One final benefit of the adoption of a flat tax would be to advance a cleaner, more ethical government. The insider circles in Washington revolve largely around money. Campaign contributions all too frequently lead to special financial favors from the government.

Lobbyists who secure special tax avoidance devices for their clients play the money game well. But while such tactics may advance the bottom line of their clients, they do little to advance the general welfare of Americans. Moreover, when money is traded for political favors in the tax arena, it becomes more likely that it will be traded for political favors in other arenas as well.

CONCLUSION

Much of what goes on in Washington may be legally correct, but it is morally degrading. A flat tax, by removing one significant source of unethical governance, could lead to unexpected benefits that come when our government does what is right.

Linda Chavez is President of the Center for Equal Opportunity in Washington, D.C. Previously, she served as White House Director of Public Liaison and Director of the U.S. Commission on Civil Rights. She is the author of *Out of the Barrio: Toward a New Politics of Hispanic Assimilation*, which chronicles the untold story of Hispanic achievement and addresses the implication of bilingual education, voting rights, immigration, and affirmative action. Along with a syndicated column, she has written for *The Wall Street Journal*, *The Washington Post*, *The New Republic*, *Commentary*, and *Reader's Digest*. Ms. Chavez received her B.A. degree from the University of Colorado.

9

WHY TAX REFORM IS GOOD FOR WOMEN

Linda Chavez
President, Center for Equal Opportunity
Former Director, U.S. Commission on Civil Rights

The status of women in America has undergone a radical transformation since women earned the right to vote in 1920. No longer are women merely economic appendages of their husbands; now they are fully independent economic beings, with all the privileges and responsibilities that this entails. Among the least pleasant of their newfound duties, women now find themselves bearing an ever-increasing share of the burden inflicted by a tax system that is progressive in name only.

How the current tax system hurts women—and their families—is a largely untold story. But first, some history.

Women's labor force participation has gone up rapidly in the past 60 years. In 1940, just 26 percent of women participated in the labor force. By 1995, the number had risen to 59 percent. And by 1996, more than 70 percent of women between the ages of 20 and 54 were wage earners, according to Diana Furchtgott Roth and Christine Stolba, authors of *Women's Figures: The Economic Progress of Women in America.*

The increase in work force participation among married women is even more dramatic. In 1920, only 9 percent of married women worked outside of the home. Thirty years later, that number had climbed to a modest 25 percent. But today, over 60 percent of married women provide family income. Working in the market economy is now the norm for American women.

Moreover, women's wages have increased relative to those of men. Contrary to popular reporting, women have nearly closed the notorious wage gap. June O'Neill, former director of the Congressional Budget Office, has reported that when earnings comparisons are based on men and women with similar experience and backgrounds, the income differential is insignificant. Among men and women ages 27 to 33 who never had a child, for instance, women's earnings are 98.1 percent of men's income.

The economic success women have achieved carries with it a curse. It means that, increasingly, they are exposed to the horrors of the tax code. They are penalized by high tax rates. Their ability to accumulate wealth is undermined by multiple taxes on savings and investment. Female-owned businesses are faced with nightmarish complexity.

Of course, these features of the tax code are equal-opportunity roadblocks to the American dream. They apply to anyone who contributes to our nation's prosperity. Some features of the tax code, however, are especially injurious to women. The marriage penalty adversely affects many working women, for instance, punishing them for entering the work force. On the other hand, because of high levels of taxation and the fact that the tax code lowers wages by overtaxing capital, many women who would rather care for their children are forced into the work force simply to help their families make ends meet.

This is why the flat tax would be good news for women. It would dramatically boost opportunities for women to advance. Even better, a fair and simple tax code would give women greater flexibility to pursue options that some of them may prefer—including the ability to devote more time to caring for their children. This chapter examines the ways in which a flat tax would benefit women as consumers, wage earners, entrepreneurs, and mothers.

WHERE ARE THE FEMINISTS?

Ironically, despite clear evidence of the increasing ability of American women to harvest the fruits of capitalism, feminists continue to assume that women are not capable of succeeding. Class and gender warfare strategies continue to dominate modern feminist discussions. Witness the recently published *Reader's Companion to U.S. Women's History*, edited by, among others, feminist Gloria Steinem. Regarding Marxism, the textbook explains, "The significant and continuing contribution of Marxist feminism is its identification of women's institutionalized and historic oppression with the system of capitalism."

The 1995 United Nations report, *Women: Looking Beyond 2000*, takes a similar view. Urging world governments to address "the question of financial resources and arrangements" so that women are "equal, active stakeholders and decision makers in the private sector, just as they must be in the public sector," the report declares that "Governments, despite their constrained resources, will need to commit themselves to further assistance."

This is clearly policy-speak for redistribution. In other words, women can advance only if they are backed by government coercion. Not surprisingly, free-market reforms that would benefit women as consumers, wage earners, and entrepreneurs are continually ignored in traditional feminist circles.

As long as feminists get to define women's interests, it will be assumed that women benefit from income redistribution and progressive taxation. At the heart of the argument is the belief that women, as a class, require the powers of government to wrest wealth away from the male ruling class. Refining the Marxist axiom, "From each according to his abilities, to each according to his needs," defenders claim that systematic discrimination impedes women's success in the marketplace. Only the benevolent generosity of an all-knowing federal government can right the wrongs inflicted by a system designed by and for men.

Even if this were true, however, it would be self-defeating. Steeply progressive tax rates do not mean more money, especially from high-income taxpayers who have access to good lawyers, lobbyists, and accountants. Instead of paying the tax collector, these people find clever ways to hide their money. Not only does the hoped-for taxation fail to generate much money, but the economy suffers because resources are being shifted away from productive uses in order to avoid excessive taxation.

The second argument for progressive taxation assumes that systematic discrimination lowers the buying power of women as a class. Government spending programs, financed by progressive taxation, are needed to supply goods and services women cannot afford as individual consumers. But even if one were to accept the premise that discrimination depresses women's wages, it is unclear why further depressing women's after-tax income, real wages, savings, and entrepreneurial opportunities is the answer.

THE TAX CODE'S ASSAULT ON WORKING WOMEN

Ironically, many of those who claim to speak for women advocate a tax system that impedes the economic progress of women, discriminates among different groups of women, and even discourages women's labor force participation. Nowhere is this more evident than in the marriage penalty tax. Thanks largely to rising tax rates, married couples are subject to higher tax burdens than are two single people with an equal combined income. The penalty is especially harsh if husbands and wives have similar incomes.

In a 1997 study of marriage and the federal income tax, the Congressional Budget Office found startling evidence of how the tax system discriminates against women. According to the CBO report, the marriage penalty has grown as a direct result of the sharp increase in women's economic participation over the past 30 years. Between 1969 and 1995, the proportion of working-age married couples grew to 72 percent. By itself, that shift tended to increase marriage penalties. Further compounding the problem, the greater equality of spouses' earnings increased both the number of couples incurring marriage penalties and the size of those penalties.

"[T]he greater equality of spouses' earnings increased both the number of couples incurring marriage penalties and the size of those penalties."

The CBO estimates that the average marriage penalty incurred by joint filers is roughly $1,400. If each spouse contributes $37,500 to the household income, together they incur a marriage penalty of $1,391. This is money they would be able to keep if they were living together and filing separately.

Because this increased burden on married couples reduces incentive, it should come as no surprise that the marriage penalty depresses labor force participation among married women. In an international comparison, economist Siv Gustafson found that when Sweden lifted its joint filing requirement for married couples, married women's participation in the labor force rose from 53 percent in 1969 to 74 percent just one decade later.

Moreover, although the tax on marriage does not appear to influence marriage rates, the CBO reports that some marriage ceremonies are put on hold in order to avoid the tax bite in a

Chart 9.1

Additional Tax on Married Couple

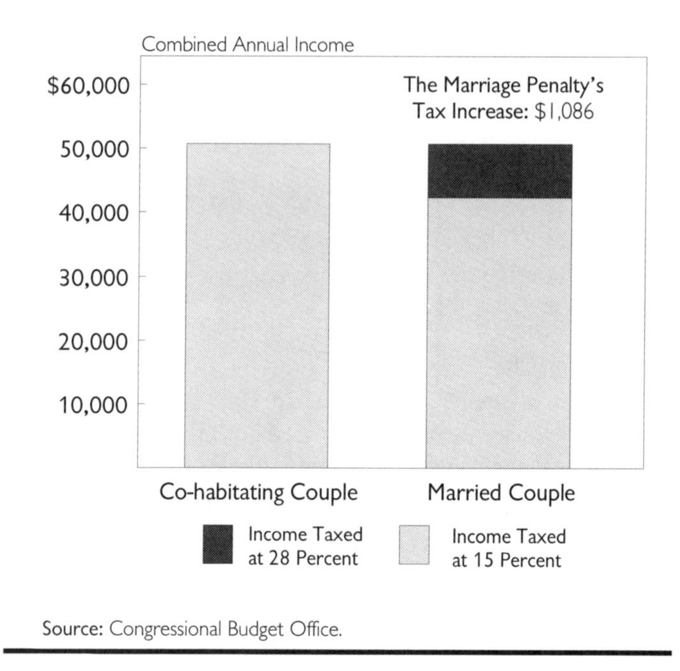

Source: Congressional Budget Office.

given year—a prime example of how the personal becomes political.

Thirty years have passed since Betty Friedan mythologized the malaise of the suburban housewife in her 1963 best-seller, *The Feminine Mystique*. In that time, women's wages have become a much more prominent share of family income. Women also are earning their fair share—something even Friedan admitted in a National Press Club gathering last fall. The current tax system, however, remains trapped in the past, treating women as dependents. Three decades out of date, and after taking billions of dollars from women's pocketbooks, the progressive tax code should be retired.

THE TAX CODE'S ASSAULT ON STAY-AT-HOME MOMS

Ironically, but perhaps not surprisingly, the current tax code buffets women from several directions. While the marriage penalty often drives women out of the labor force by taxing their income at very high rates, as just discussed, there also are many women who would prefer to devote a portion of their lives to taking care of their children but instead are forced into the labor force because of the tax code.

Part of the problem is high levels of taxation. The seizure of more and more family income by the IRS forces some women to work outside the home simply to make ends meet. Their husband's after-tax income falls short of their family bills.

Compounding this effect is the fact that the tax code's bias against savings and investment reduces wage growth and makes it harder to support a family on one income. As every economist knows, raising productivity through capital investment is the key to raising real wages—money to pay for food, clothes, shelter, or a college education, to replace an old washing machine, or simply to take the family on a camping trip.

This "double whammy"—driving women into the workforce and then overtaxing them—creates more dependence on government over the long term. In effect, many women are drawn into a vicious cycle of seeking government security to replace the income lost to government taxes. This may explain the more statist voting behavior and public opinions expressed by females.

Would it not be better if the tax code were reformed so that the government was not forcing women into unpalatable choices? A flat tax, by imposing only one low tax rate and getting rid of all bias against savings and investment, would create more prosperity and lift wages. This would allow women to make economic choices that truly matched their preferences and desires. Under a flat tax, instead of being dragged into or forced out of the labor market by socially engineered tax policy, women would be able to decide for themselves.

PROMOTING THE GENERAL WELFARE

Whether she is a single mother, stay-at-home mom, recent college graduate, or business entrepreneur, every woman stands to benefit from a simple and fair flat tax. A flat tax would boost disposable income for families by reducing the tax burden and by increasing economic growth.

In a study for the National Center for Policy Analysis (NCPA), economists Barry J. Seldon of the University of Texas and Roy G. Boyd of Ohio University calculated that a 17 percent flat tax would increase production in every industry except financial services. The greatest increase would be in savings, which Seldon and Boyd predict would grow by 7.4 percent, further spurring investment activity. Because of added wealth and higher incomes, the consumption of housing, food, clothing, automobiles, and consumer services would increase under a flat tax.

"Whether she is a single mother, stay-at-home mom, recent college graduate, or business entrepreneur, every woman stands to benefit from a simple and fair flat tax."

High tax rates hinder growth, but the damage can be undone. Indeed, this is the lesson of the Kennedy tax cuts in the 1960s and the Reagan tax cuts in the 1980s. Contrary to what class-warfare demagogues claimed would happen, the economy boomed. Nobel Prize-winning economist Robert E. Lucas of the University of Chicago puts it this way in a Federal Reserve publication: "The supply side economists...have delivered the largest genuinely free lunch that I have seen in 25 years in this business and I believe that we would have a better society if we followed their advice."

The bias against savings in the tax code harms women in their relatively new role as employers. The National Foundation of Women Business Owners estimates that women own 7.7 million businesses in the United States, employing 15.5 million workers. Women own 3.5 million home-based businesses, concentrated largely in service-oriented industries such as finance and consulting. The Department of Labor's *1993 Handbook on Women Workers* documents that women are starting businesses at twice the rate of men. A tax system that does not discriminate against savings and investment will help make capital more available to these entrepreneurs. They also will benefit from a flat tax because of the reduction in tax compliance costs.

Under the 17 percent flat tax proposal introduced by House Majority Leader Richard Armey (R–TX) and Senator Richard Shelby (R–AL) during the 105th Congress, Seldon and Boyd find that "among all income groups, the lowest-income Americans will gain the most in percentage terms." The estimated 7.6 percent increase in disposable income for those earning $0 to $9,999 annually is attributable to the generous personal allowances carved out in the Armey–Shelby bill.

This has particular significance for women. In 1990, women were 51.3 percent of the population, yet they accounted for 57.7 percent of all persons living in poverty. According to the *1993 Handbook on Women Workers*, from 1970 to 1990, female-headed households accounted for 99 percent of the increase in those living in poverty. For a single working mother on the lowest rungs of the economic ladder, an increase in disposable income would increase her ability to keep her family afloat. And should she decide to marry at some future point, a flat tax—unlike the current progressive system—would not punish her choice.

COMPLEXITY: MAKING PAYING TAXES MORE PAINFUL

When first enacted by Congress in 1913, the federal income tax required a two-page form with two pages of instructions. *The New York Times* published the tax forms on a single news page. Difficult as it is for modern taxpayers to imagine, the top tax rate was 7 percent. And that rate applied only to the wealthiest members of society.

"Americans spend a staggering 5.4 billion hours filling out tax forms—more than the number of hours spent to build every car, van, truck, and airplane in the United States."

Today, the tax code has ballooned to over 17,000 pages of rules, regulations, and loopholes. Americans spend a staggering 5.4 billion hours filling out tax forms—more than the number of hours spent to build every car, van, truck, and airplane in the United States. The Internal Revenue Service estimates that a 1040 form (supposedly "E-Z") requires 653 minutes to complete.

Time spent sorting through the 569 tax forms, trying to reach one of over 100,000 IRS employees for assistance, and reading through reams of complicated tax rules is time that could be infinitely better spent. Overworked mothers would rather be doing something else for their children.

Not surprisingly, many taxpayers in desperation seek the help of professionals. Americans spend roughly $30 billion per year on tax preparers. And lest one think tax accountants are a luxury enjoyed by the rich, consider: Two-thirds of professionally prepared tax returns are filed by Americans with yearly incomes below $50,000, according to Stephen Moore's 1995 book, *The Economic and Civil Liberties Case for a National Sales Tax.*

The Tax Foundation, a nonprofit watchdog group, estimates that the total cost of income tax compliance is roughly $150 billion. Some estimates put the number as high as $200 billion. The expense imposed on families to comply with the current tangle of tax regulations is a burden and a drain. A simple postcard-size return would go a long way toward alleviating tax-time pressures.

ENOUGH IS ENOUGH

Even more onerous than the burden of filling out the tax forms, however, are the direct and indirect costs of the record-high taxes we now pay. After nearly 100 years of political manipulation, Americans are saddled with a tax system that inhibits economic growth, distorts the supply of goods and services, and reduces disposable income. Excessive taxation undermines prosperity for all, but women are particularly vulnerable because they do not have as much experience in the work force.

Taking More of What We Earn. In his 1996 testimony before the House Ways and Means Committee explaining his 17 percent flat tax proposal, Representative Armey noted that the typical family must pay 24.5 percent of their income to the tax collector—and that is just for income and payroll taxes. Marginal tax rates (the percentage of each added dollar of income) are even higher. Middle-class families often face a 28 percent tax rate on additional income. Adding payroll and state taxes, the marginal tax rate could easily reach over 50 percent.

As recently as last September, economists Patrick Fleenor and Scott Moody of the Tax Foundation found that federal, state, and local taxes in 1998 amounted to $9,939 per capita, with $6,810 of this amount going to the federal government. In dramatic comparison, the Tax Foundation reports that this is more than Americans will spend on food, clothing, shelter, and transportation combined.

Confiscatory tax rates do not reflect American values. A 1995 *Reader's Digest* poll found that, when asked to name the highest total tax that families of four should pay, respondents across economic, racial, and ideological lines answered with astounding unanimity: The government should take no more than 25 percent. It is worth underscoring that 25 percent covers all federal, state, and local taxes. Indeed, taxes may be the one area in which President Bill Clinton turns a deaf ear to the polls, as evidenced by his 1993 tax hike.

Reducing What We Earn. Not only does the current tax code take too much of our money, but it also reduces the amount we earn. A progressive tax structure combined with double taxation of savings and investment prevents resources from flowing to their most productive uses. It punishes economic success, distorts economic decisions, and misallocates capital investment. The result: Workers are denied full technological advances that otherwise would increase their productivity, real wages, and standard of living. This has particular consequence for women who, as a group, have been the biggest beneficiaries of the growth in the white-collar sector.

An NCPA study conducted last year by Gerald Scully, a University of Texas economist, estimates that excessive tax rates between 1950 and 1995 reduced the annual growth in gross domestic product (GDP) by 1.4 percent. This may not sound like much, but it translates into thousands and thousands of dollars in lost income each year, and workers with more income no longer would feel compelled to support costly government programs.

CONCLUSION

> We are persons; native, free-born citizens; property-holders, tax-payers, yet we are denied the

> exercise of our public right to the elective franchise.... True, the unmarried woman has a right to the property she inherits and the money she earns, but she is taxed without representation.

It has been nearly 150 years since Elizabeth Cady Stanton delivered these prescient words to the New York legislature. Unfortunately, modern feminism has undermined the campaign for individual economic sovereignty, choosing instead to favor redistributive policies that ultimately increase women's economic dependence.

It is a measure of how far feminism has veered from its original meritocratic roots that democratic capitalism, championed by Stanton and her fellow suffragettes, is regarded by many of today's feminist policymakers as inimical to women's progress. Tax reform may not seem to be a gender issue, but as Stanton's words make clear, taxes are a women's issue—now more than ever.

The time has come to liberate women from the yoke of unfair taxation. Indeed, one of the best reasons to reform the tax code is that women are punished no matter what they do. The infamous marriage penalty discriminates against working women, punishing wives with punitive tax rates. Yet the current system also harms stay-at-home moms—the tax code's bias against capital formation is slowing wage growth, and making it harder to support a family on one income.

"Tax reform may not seem to be a gender issue, but as Stanton's words make clear, taxes are a women's issue.... Simply put, women cannot afford current tax policies—in time or in dollars."

Simply put, women cannot afford current tax policies—in time or in dollars. That is why we need the flat tax.

Dean R. Kleckner has served as President of the American Farm Bureau Federation since 1986. He operates a 350-acre corn, soybean, and hog farm near Rudd, Iowa. A strong advocate of reduced protectionism and free trade, Mr. Kleckner served as the only farmer on the U.S. advisory team to the General Agreement on Tariffs and Trade when trade negotiations began in September 1986. He continues to serve on the U.S. Trade Advisory Committee, first appointed by President Reagan and re-appointed by Presidents Bush and Clinton. In 1995, he was appointed to the National Commission on Economic Growth and Tax Reform. From 1988 to 1989, he served on the National Economic Commission, which advised the President and Congress on ways to reduce the federal budget deficit while promoting economic growth.

10

WHY FARMERS AND RANCHERS NEED TAX REFORM

Dean R. Kleckner
President, American Farm Bureau Federation

Farmers and ranchers clearly need tax reform. Like other small and medium-size business owners, they are frustrated by high tax rates, the complexity of the tax code, the continuous changes made in the code, and the taxation of income two, three, or even four times. But they also view tax reform on a much more personal level.

Many of America's farms and ranches have been family operations for generations, some for more than 100 years. According to the 1997 Census of Agriculture, 86 percent of farms and ranches are individual or family proprietorships, and nearly 9 percent are partnerships. Family corporations (most with ten or fewer stockholders) make up most of the rest of farm and ranch operations. These families want a code that does not penalize their savings and investments, and they want the estate tax elimi-

"These families want a code that does not penalize their savings and investments, and they want the estate tax eliminated so their farms and ranches can be passed to the next generation."

nated so their farms and ranches can be passed to the next generation.

Farm and ranch income, by nature, tends to vary greatly from year to year. Weather changes and shifting market conditions produce large swings in output and prices. Compared with people who have more stable incomes, farmers and ranchers are at a disadvantage; the current system, with its many tax brackets, taxes them in good income years at substantially higher rates than if their income had been more stable from year to year.

Congress has tried to deal with this by allowing three-year partial income averaging. Although this is helpful, it also makes the tax system even more complex and leaves many unanswered questions about the alternative minimum tax and other elements of the tax code.

All of these tax problems must be considered in light of the need to simplify the tax code and make it as permanent as public policy can be. This is why fundamental reform is more desirable than incremental change.

Policymakers have made ad hoc changes over the years to benefit farmers and ranchers, but this approach made the tax code more and more complex. Moreover, positive changes made one year are offset by tax increases in other years. This destructive cycle must be broken. Farmers and ranchers need "tax policy certainty." A 25-year-old farmer or rancher looks forward to at least 40 years of productive life. Farmland is held for an average of 30 years. A tax code that changes every year or two is incompatible with those planning horizons.

Tax reform, therefore, must not be a temporary or quick fix. It must involve long-term, fundamental change. Regardless of whether the final reform focuses on the flat tax or on a national sales tax, long-term changes that simplify the process must be the cornerstones of the new tax policy.

Tax reform should also provide some protection for taxpayers who made decisions under the old system. Simply stated, if individuals, farmers, businessmen, or ranchers enter into contracts with the promise of a certain tax treatment, it would not be proper to pull the rug out from under them. This is true even if some of the tax breaks they are using will not be available under something like a flat tax. (For instance, current homeowners could deduct interest for existing mortgages, but new home buyers—who would borrow at much lower interest rates and therefore would not need the deduction—could not). Not only is this fair, but it is smart politics because it takes an argument away from interest-group opponents of tax reform.

THE BENEFITS OF A SINGLE-RATE INCOME TAX

There are two versions of a single-rate income tax: the flat tax and the "consumed-income" tax. Both proposals would integrate business and personal income taxes into one system and tax all income at the same single rate. Both approaches would result in a consumption-based system, ending the double taxation of savings and investment. And both of these taxes would not only simplify the tax system, but also eliminate the estate tax and capital gains tax, which are of great concern to farmers and ranchers. Tax planning would become less important, so people would be able to spend more time creating wealth and building businesses.

The flat tax has been popularized by Republican presidential candidate Steve Forbes and House Majority Leader Richard Armey (R–TX). It is the best-known tax reform plan under consideration. It would tax wages, salaries, and pensions at the individual level and tax all other income at the business level. Any income that is taxed once under this system could not be taxed again. The consumed-income approach is also a flat tax, but it gets rid of the double taxation of savings by creating a universal and unlimited individual retirement account (IRA).

Both approaches would leave the self-employment and payroll taxes for Social Security and Medicare untouched. Although reforming these programs would have additional benefits, trying to change too much of the current system at one time could doom the entire tax reform effort.

How Farmers and Ranchers Would Benefit

The Armey and Forbes versions of the flat tax, which grabbed the most attention in the tax reform debate and offer dramatic tax reform, would not require farmers and ranchers to learn an entirely new way to pay their taxes. Instead, it is a greatly simplified income tax that is designed to be fair and pro-growth.

What does this mean for the agricultural community? Gross income would change very little. Sales of crops and livestock produced on the farm and income from custom harvesting and other similar activities would be treated the same as they are under current law.

Most operating expenses would continue to be treated as they are under current law, including the deductibility of such expenses as feed, livestock, or poultry purchased for resale, seed, fertilizer, lime, fuels, pesticides, repairs, maintenance, machine hire, custom work, marketing, storage, transportation, and rent to landlords. These expenses account for about two-thirds of total farm production expenses as measured by the U.S. Department of Agriculture.

Any Changes? One big change is that capital sales would not be treated as income unless the taxpayer was allowed to deduct the original purchase price of the asset. Another change is that interest expenses would no longer be deductible. In 1998, interest expenses for farmers and ranchers amounted to about $13.5 billion, or 7.3 percent of total expenses.

Under current law, the tax system incorporates a bias in favor of debt capital and against equity capital, since interest is deductible and dividends are not. One way to remove that bias would be to make interest non-deductible, an approach taken by the Armey and Forbes flat tax proposals. (An alternative would make both interest and dividends deductible.) To provide consistency, all businesses, whether sole proprietorships, partnerships, or corporations, would receive equal treatment.

Hired labor is another area in which changes would occur with these reforms. Under current law, wages, fringe benefits, and payroll taxes are deductible by employers. Wages are taxable income to employees, but fringe benefits are not. This creates a bias for fringe benefits over cash wages.

To have a unified tax system, items that are deductible for employers must be taxable income to employees, and items that are not deductible to employers must not be taxable to employees. This would ensure that all income is taxed once, but only once, and that the tax system does not bias economic decision-making. Farmers and ranchers generally would prefer to pay cash wages and not try to become experts on fringe benefits, especially since they often deal with a transitory workforce. This change in the tax code would lessen their paperwork burden and reduce the complexity of the current tax system.

State and local property taxes are a third category of operating expense where changes would occur. Under current law, property taxes are deductible as a business expense. The flat tax would eliminate the deductibility of state and local taxes. This would have a substantial impact on farmers and ranchers who have large amounts of land in areas where property taxes are high and the returns to the land are relatively low. It likely would fuel attempts to do away with property taxes for the government financing of schools.

The current tax system also requires that investment expenses be depreciated over time, even though the cost is incurred when the asset is purchased. This both biases the code against investment and adds to its complexity. The flat tax would provide for direct expensing of capital assets in the year purchased, with a carry-forward provision if needed. Depreciation adds complexity to the tax code for farmers and ranchers, while direct expensing simplifies the tax system. Direct expensing also would provide significant short-term benefits to farming and ranching operations that invest heavily in capital assets. In the long run, however, these capital assets must be financially productive or the money would be wasted.

It should be obvious that taxing all income at a single low rate would be good news, particularly since it protects farmers and ranchers with variable income from being punished by higher tax rates.

The Consumed-Income Tax Approach

Under a consumed-income flat tax, any income that is saved is not taxed. This is like a traditional IRA. (The Armey/Forbes flat tax is like the new back-ended, or Roth, IRA.) Any withdrawals from this unlimited IRA, however, must be included as part of taxable income; this means that the original income is taxed along with any earnings.

All taxation under a consumed-income tax occurs at the individual level, so dividends, interest, and profits would be deductible to the business and taxable to individuals. This, of course, is the opposite of the Armey/Forbes flat tax, which taxes all income at the business level and spares individuals from having to pay another layer of tax on that income.

Like the well-known flat tax, the consumed-income approach eliminates the need to find tax shelters for savings. It eliminates concerns about estate taxes, capital gains taxes on savings, and transfers of assets at retirement. It does little to simplify the tax code, except to replace depreciation with expensing.

THE IMPACT OF A NATIONAL SALES TAX

A national sales tax that replaced the income tax, capital gains tax, and estate tax—and possibly self-employment and payroll taxes for Social Security and Medicare—could eliminate federal tax problems for farmers and ranchers or add to them, depending on how it was administered. A true national retail sales tax that applied only to the final retail sale would remove most farmers and ranchers from the federal tax process. Only about 5 percent of farmers and ranchers market directly to consumers, so only they would have to collect the tax.

Since a national retail sales tax probably would have to be relatively high to generate revenue in amounts similar to those produced by current federal taxes, the potential for tax evasion also could be high. Supporters of the "FairTax" national sales tax estimate that a 23 percent national retail sales tax (30 percent if measured the traditional way) would be needed to replace the current federal estate tax, individual and corporate income taxes, the capital gains tax, and payroll taxes. Combined with local and state sales taxes, the total retail sales tax could approach 35 percent or more in some states.

Federal sales tax authorities likely would require some type of reporting by farmers and ranchers to ensure that they are not evading the tax by selling to consumers and failing to report such sales. Those who do sell directly to consumers would face scrutiny to ensure that they are not evading tax collection.

A national retail sales tax would exempt farm and ranch inputs, including inputs purchased from businesses that sell to retail customers. This would require a close review of records to root out tax evasion. For example, since the parts needed to repair a pickup truck used in agricultural production are the same as the parts needed to repair a pickup truck used for pleasure, documentation that they were used in production would be required to counter the potential for tax evasion. The national sales tax would have to be coordinated with the 46 states that have sales taxes. Currently, each state chooses which items to tax and how to exempt agriculture from taxation.

Chart 10.1

The Flat Tax vs. a National Sales Tax: Individuals Face One Layer of Tax When Income Is Either Earned or Spent

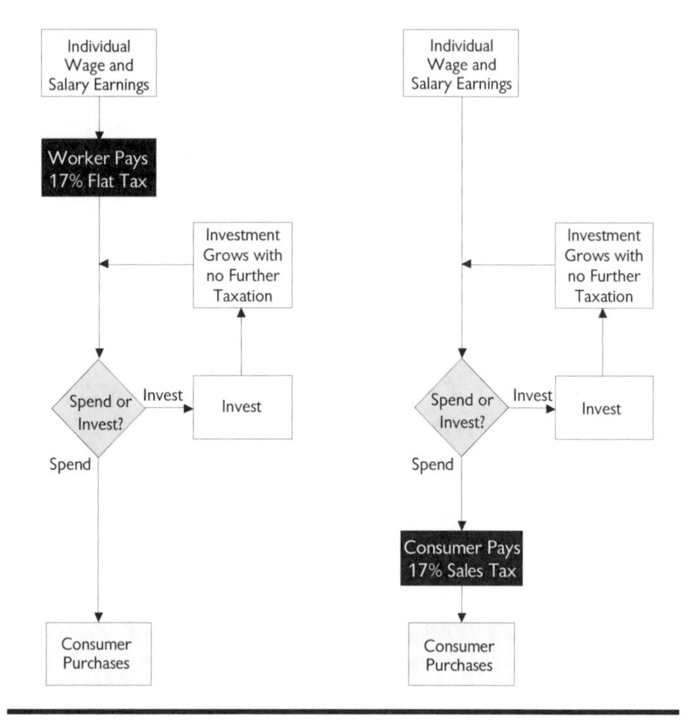

A national retail sales tax clearly would eliminate some of the taxes of greatest concern to farmers and ranchers. It also would reduce the tax compliance burden. However, new compliance costs could develop as evasion and avoidance increase in response to the high tax rates. In addition, a national sales tax could be transformed into a transaction tax that is applied to all purchases of agricultural inputs and sales of agricultural output.

MOVING TOWARD TAX REFORM

Because of their harsh impact on farmers and ranchers, who often are cash-poor but land-rich, it is worth spending some extra time on two of the worst parts of the current tax code: the estate tax (better known as the death tax) and the capital gains tax.

The Estate Tax

The estate tax is clearly at the top of farmers' reform list. It strikes at the heart of the issue of transferring the ownership of a multi-generation family farm from one generation to the next. About 14 percent of agricultural estates grossing $50,000 or more per year owe estate taxes, compared with only about 1 percent of all other estates.

The current estate tax ranges from 37 percent for taxable estates valued at $650,000 to 55 percent for estates valued above $3 million. Estates that do not owe taxes are still required to prepare the paperwork in order to verify that determination. Consequently, many farm and ranch families incur thousands of dollars in estate planning expenses in order to minimize or avoid this confiscatory tax; otherwise, the number of farms owing estate taxes would be even higher.

"The estate tax is clearly at the top of farmers' reform list. It strikes at the heart of the issue of transferring the ownership of a multi-generation family farm from one generation to the next."

Congress has made good-faith efforts over the years to lessen the impact of estate taxes by creating such features of the code as a family-owned business exemption of $1.3 million and the valuation of land assets at productive value rather than market value. Although these changes in tax law have been helpful, they also have added to the complexity and uncertainty of the tax code. Any serious tax reform should eliminate estate taxes as part of the overall effort to implement a far simpler tax code—one that does not put farmers and ranchers at a disadvantage.

Capital Gains Taxes

After eliminating estate taxes, the next step for Congress should be to eliminate capital gains taxes. Capital gains taxes do not tax income; they tax the transfer of assets from one form to another. This discourages farmers and ranchers from selling their assets even when it makes good economic sense for them to do so. Selling some farmland and using the money to expand a livestock operation may make good economic sense, for instance, but the capital gains tax discourages such a transfer.

Capital gains taxes hurt farmers and ranchers at retirement as well. Farm and ranch business assets often are the substance of a family's retirement plan. They represent a lifetime of saving and investing. Yet when assets are sold to move money into other assets that are more appropriate for guaranteeing income during retirement, the federal government taxes that transfer. This unfairly affects farmers and ranchers, compared with people who have been allowed to build up their assets in company-sponsored pension plans, 401(k) plans, and IRAs.

CONCLUSION

The need for fundamental tax reform for farmers and ranchers is clear and urgent. Congress has struggled with this issue for over 20 years, and it had some successes and some failures in the 1986 tax reform legislation. Some of the piecemeal changes in recent years have been good for some farmers and ranchers, but they also have created an even more complex tax code.

Farmers and ranchers need specific tax changes, such as the elimination of the estate and capital gains taxes and the enactment of lower tax rates to address variability of income. Tax reforms that do not deal effectively with these issues are incomplete. Tax reductions that add to the complexity of the code are a mixed blessing. Making many small cuts while leaving the current tax structure intact and available for future tax increases should be discouraged.

Now is the time to make fundamental, long-lasting changes. The 25-year-old new farmer and the 60-year-old farming or ranching parents who want to begin easing out of day-to-day operations should not be held in tax policy limbo. Whether the changes can be accomplished in one major tax reform or must be implemented one step at a time is not the key issue. The key issue is fixing the current system, which is too complex and unfair.

Elaine L. Chao, a Distinguished Fellow at The Heritage Foundation, served as President and CEO of United Way of America from 1992 to 1996. Under her leadership, dramatic reforms were instituted that earned the public's trust, and overall fundraising by local United Ways achieved new levels. Before joining United Way, Ms. Chao was Deputy Secretary of the U.S. Department of Transportation and Director of the Peace Corps, the world's largest international volunteer organization. In 1988 and 1989, she chaired the Federal Maritime Commission. With a background in international banking and finance, Ms. Chao was Vice President for syndications at BankAmerica Capital Markets Groups in San Francisco from 1984 to 1986. She received her M.B.A. from Harvard Business School.

11

WHY THE FLAT TAX WILL BOOST CHARITABLE GIVING

Elaine L. Chao
Distinguished Fellow, The Heritage Foundation
Former President and CEO, United Way of America

One of the most controversial aspects of the flat tax is the elimination of the deduction for charitable contributions. Yet concerns that tax reform will harm charities are unwarranted. Data from the government and the nonprofit sector indicate that giving to charities will increase with the passage of a pure flat tax. The reason: The flat tax will increase economic growth, personal income, savings, and net wealth, all of which lead to higher levels of giving.

Upon further reflection, these findings should not come as a surprise. Americans have always helped their neighbors in need. Charitable giving blossomed before there ever was an income tax, and donations remain strong today, even from the more than 70 percent of taxpayers who do not itemize and therefore get no benefit from the deduction.

> *"The flat tax will increase economic growth, personal income, savings, and net wealth, all of which lead to higher levels of giving."*

Advocates for nonprofit organizations are certainly right to worry about changes in tax policy. Some changes, such as eliminating the deduction *without* the accompanying reforms to boost economic growth, would cause donations to fall. This would be a mistake—especially if, as most conservatives believe, charitable institutions should take a more prominent role in providing social safety nets.

The flat tax is good for charities, by contrast, because it will eliminate features of the tax code that hinder economic expansion, wealth creation, and income growth. And with a bigger pie, charitable organizations are sure to get a bigger slice. Specifically:

- **Increased personal income leads to increased donations.** The single greatest determinant of the level of overall charitable giving in our country every year is the state of the economy and people's perceived sense of their own financial security and net worth. In this decade alone, a weak domestic economy during the early 1990s yielded near stagnant levels of growth in annual giving levels. As the economy picked up steam, however, the level of charitable contributions increased dramatically.
- **Donations as a percentage of personal income have remained constant, despite wide variations in the income tax.** Although the top marginal income tax rate—and therefore the value of the deduction—has varied from 28 percent to 91 percent during the post-World War II era, the amount that individuals donate to nonprofit organizations has remained relatively constant, at around 1.8 percent of personal income.
- **Other factors besides taxes determine how much an individual donates to charitable organizations.** Various surveys indicate that marital status, religious participation, age, and whether a person is asked to give are all factors that significantly affect the amount an individual donates to charity.

These factors lie largely outside the income tax structure and have little to do with tax preferences or whether the federal income tax is flat.

Retaining the charitable deduction as part of a flat tax would prevent reformers from achieving the underlying goal of a flat tax—which is to make the federal income tax system fair and less intrusive by taxing all income at one low rate, and only once. Any proposed change in the tax system should be measured against this standard.

Retaining the charitable deduction in particular would have several detrimental effects:

1. **A higher tax rate for all taxpayers.** Allowing the deduction would necessitate imposing a higher rate even on those with lower incomes.
2. **The possibility of other deductions.** The best excuse for creating another deduction is the existence of another one—and the next one might not be as admirable as a charitable deduction.
3. **The promotion of federal social engineering.** The current tax code arbitrarily encourages certain behaviors and discourages others. Retaining any deductions under a flat tax, including the charitable contribution deduction, would continue this practice.

"The best excuse for creating another deduction is the existence of another one—and the next one might not be as admirable as a charitable deduction."

The debate over the charitable deduction, and whether or not to retain it under a flat tax, has generated a great deal of lobbying activity by non-profit organizations that fear their financial base is at risk. To understand why this fear is unjustified, it is important to understand which organizations benefit from this deduction today.

WHAT IS A NONPROFIT?

Generally, nonprofit organizations are tax-exempt entities that provide a service or good without profit as the primary motivation. Within this general classification exist a great variety of organizations, from soup kitchens and homeless shelters, to art galleries and symphony orchestras, to political parties and campaigns.

By this general definition, nonprofits have existed throughout American history. As J. Gregory Dees, a professor at the Harvard Business School, notes in "The Social Enterprise Spectrum: Philanthropy to Commerce,"

> Throughout history, private parties have organized for the purpose of promoting the common good, serving the needy, or providing goods and services that were not, in their judgment, being adequately or appropriately provided by either business or government.

However, it was not until 1917—when Congress and President Woodrow Wilson passed the deduction for charitable contributions—that the nonprofit sector became entwined with the tax system. Since then, it has been necessary for the federal government to decide which organizations legally should be considered nonprofits and therefore worthy of special treatment in the tax code.

What has emerged is a hodgepodge of organizations that may classify as nonprofits under the general definition but may be ineligible for favorable tax treatment because the federal government determined that their activities are not of special value. For example, donations made to political campaigns (clearly nonprofit) are not tax deductible, while donations to hospitals (despite the high salaries of administrators and doctors) do receive the tax break.

The legal definition of nonprofits has become even hazier over the past ten years, as many organizations that traditionally depend on charitable donations for their operation are now engaged in commercial activities. Hospitals are one example. Another is the soup kitchen that operates a for-profit restaurant to train homeless individuals in work skills and to subsidize the organization's charitable functions.

Even within individual classifications, there is a wide diversity of nonprofit organizations. For example, the College Democrats, the University of Notre Dame, and Sidwell Friends Middle School are all categorized as "educational organizations." Similarly, The Heritage Foundation and the Brookings Institution are both classified as educational organizations, and yet are very different in outlook, structure, focus, and membership. To speak of "the nonprofits" as if they somehow constituted a single entity is therefore misleading.

The diversity of the nonprofit sector also is overlooked by many Americans who continue to think of nonprofit groups exclusively as charitable organizations whose aim is to help the disadvantaged. Yet the human service / welfare nonprofits that do fit this widely held definition received only 8.1 percent of all charitable contributions in 1996, according to *Giving USA 1997: The Annual Report on Philanthropy for the Year.*

The Importance of Religious Organizations

Another factor often overlooked is the role that religious organizations play in providing assistance to disadvantaged groups. Surveys usually determine how much money is donated to religious organizations but do not investigate how that money is used. Because donations to religious organizations represent 46.1 percent of all donations, this is a very important consideration.

A 1991 study by Virginia Hodgkinson and Murray Weitzman found that a full 91.7 percent of religious congregations in

America use a portion of their donations to sponsor human service/welfare programs. These activities range from youth groups (72.6 percent of congregations participate) and food kitchens (50.1 percent participation) to family and marriage counseling (62 percent participation).

The study, published by Independent Sector, a national coalition of voluntary organizations, foundations, and corporate giving programs that encourages philanthropy and nonprofit initiatives, also found that religious congregations donated a total of $28 billion to other charitable activities, including $11 billion in volunteer time. Their $17 billion in direct expenditures represented 31 percent of the total amount donated to religious congregations that year. In other words, nearly one-third of the money donated to religious congregations is spent on charitable activities other than religious functions.

The activities of religious congregations are an important component of human service nonprofits. As a result, if higher personal incomes cause increased donations to religious congregations, the activities these congregations sponsor will see a corresponding increase in funding.

HOW WILL THE FLAT TAX AFFECT CHARITABLE DONATIONS?

Donations to nonprofit organizations would likely increase under a flat tax with no charitable deduction. And donations to religious organizations and charitable organizations that are engaged directly in human service and welfare activities would likely increase the most. The simple reason is that under a flat tax, Americans will see an increase in economic growth, personal income, savings, and net wealth, all of which will enable them to donate more to charitable organizations.

Chart 11.1

Charitable Giving Closely Tied to Income Growth

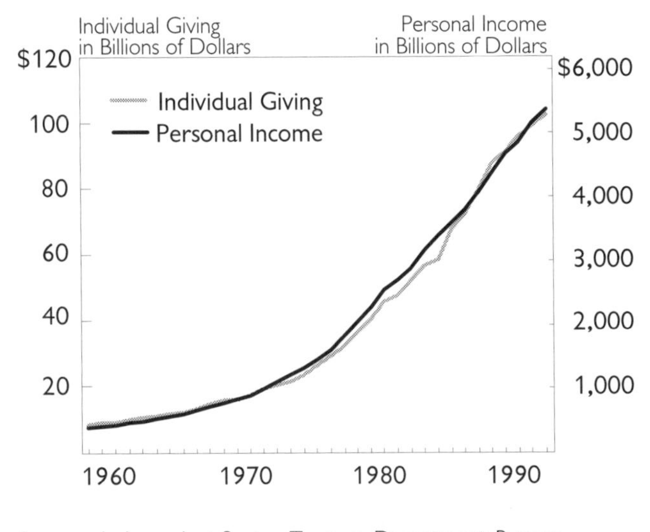

Sources: Independent Sector; Treasury Department; Bureau of Economic Affairs.

Increased Income Will Lead to Increased Donations

The more money people have at their disposal, the more they donate to charitable organizations. This obvious fact is often overlooked in the flat tax debate. A 1996 poll by Independent Sector found that individuals earning between $50,000 and $75,000 per year gave more than twice as much as individuals who earned between $40,000 and $50,000. As a result, charities have a big incentive to support policies that boost economic growth. Simply stated, the bigger the pie, the bigger their slice.

The flat tax is one of the best ways to increase personal income and wealth and to encourage economic growth—

thereby increasing charitable donations. Noted Harvard economist Dale Jorgenson has estimated that general economic activity would increase by about 10 percent with passage of a flat tax, and other economists estimate that personal income would increase by as much as 15 percent. If the share of personal income that individuals dedicate to charitable causes remains constant (and the historical evidence predicts just that), giving will increase by a similar amount.

Variations in Tax Rates Do Not Change the Percentage of Income Donated

When tax rates are reduced, the value of all itemized deductions is lowered. When the tax rate is 70 percent, for instance, it "costs" only 30 cents out-of-pocket to donate $1 to charity. If the tax rate drops to 25 percent, by contrast, the out-of-pocket cost of contributing rises to 75 cents. This, in a nutshell, is why some charities are concerned. Under a flat tax, not only is there no deduction, but it really would not matter whether one did exist because the rate would be too low for the deduction to be worth anything.

Because lower tax rates increase the after-tax cost of charitable donations, the across-the-board tax rate reductions of the 1980s caused consternation in the nonprofit community. But even though the value of the tax deduction has changed dramatically over the years, particularly in the 1980s, the level of charitable giving has remained relatively constant—around 1.8 percent of total personal income, based on *Giving USA 1997* and *Historical Statistics of the United States*. This constant level of giving has persisted despite a top marginal tax rate that has fluctuated between 28 percent and 91 percent.

The 1981 Tax Rate Cuts. In 1981, President Ronald Reagan's first economic plan became law and dramatically reduced marginal tax rates. The plan included an across-the-board reduction of 25 percent in marginal tax rates for individuals, as well as a reduction in the highest individual rate from 70 percent to 50

Chart 11.2

Falling Value of Charitable Deduction Associated with Increased Contributions

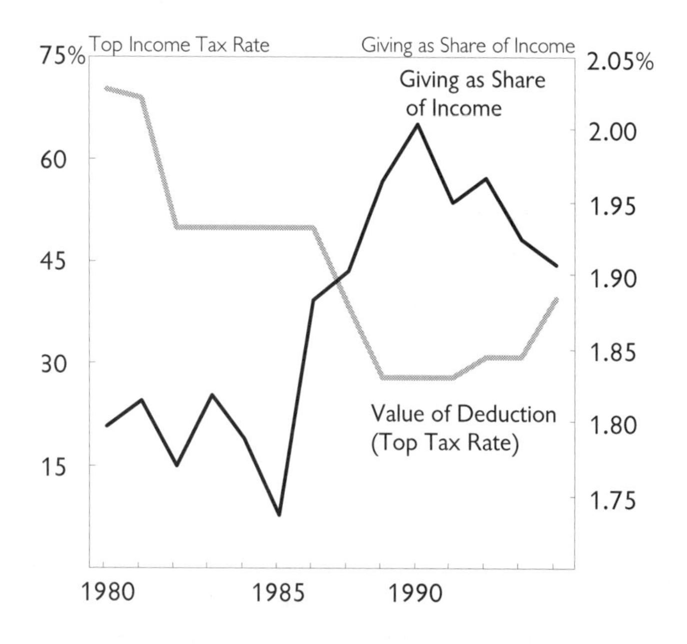

Sources: Independent Sector; Treasury Department; Bureau of Economic Affairs.

percent. Many analysts and directors of nonprofit organizations feared that a significant decrease in charitable donations would follow.

These fears were never realized. In 1986, with President Reagan's plan fully in effect, total charitable giving was 16 percent higher (after accounting for inflation) than it had been in 1980. The economic growth that resulted from reducing marginal tax rates actually boosted the amount donated to charitable organizations.

Moreover, *Giving USA 1997* reported that total giving accounted for 1.9 percent of gross domestic product in 1986, compared with only 1.7 percent in 1980. Between 1980 and 1986, the amounts contributed by donors in every category (individuals, corporations, foundations, and bequests) increased, as did the levels of contributions received by nonprofits in every category (from the arts to human service organizations).

The 1986 Tax Reform. The 1986 tax bill eliminated numerous deductions in the federal income tax code and lowered the top individual marginal tax rate from 50 percent to 28 percent. The itemized deduction for charitable giving remained, but the "above-the-line" tax deduction for charitable contributions was eliminated. This, combined with the fact that lower rates made the deduction for itemizers less valuable, substantially reduced tax preferences for charitable giving.

Because of lower marginal rates and the elimination of the above-the-line deduction, many analysts predicted a dramatic reduction in the amount of money donated to charitable organizations. For example, *Philanthropy Monthly* published an article in 1986 citing an Independent Sector report that charitable giving would decline by $8 billion because of the 1986 Tax Reform Act.

These fears were misplaced. Charitable donations for 1987 totaled $90.3 billion, a 7.6 percent increase over 1986, and total giving in 1986 amounted to $83.9 billion, a 15 percent increase over 1985. In fact, *Giving USA 1997* reported that total charitable donations increased (in inflation-adjusted terms) every year between 1983 and 1989. Far from the bleak outcome predicted by analysts, charitable contributions actually increased after enactment of the 1986 tax bill—again, as a result of strong economic growth.

There are several factors that do affect the giving pattern of individuals. However, the evidence of the past 70 years (and particularly that of the 1980s) shows that changes in the after-tax value of the charitable deduction are not among them. People give to charity because they believe in the organization to which they are giving. This does not change with reforms in the tax code.

A Flat Tax Will Stimulate More Donations

Some 46 million American households give to charities but do not claim an income tax deduction. These non-itemizers account for roughly 63.4 percent of all donors, according to Giving and Volunteering in the United States 1996. Therefore, there must be reasons other than the tax deduction that cause individuals to donate a portion of their hard-earned money to charity.

As the report noted, the following factors are directly associated with charitable giving:

- **Church attendance.** Perhaps the single most important indicator in determining an individual's level of charitable giving (to all charitable causes, not just religious congregations) is church attendance. In 1994, donors who attended church gave an average of 2.2 percent of their income to charity; those who did not attend church averaged only 1.4 percent. With specific reference to the frequency of church attendance, again in 1994, donors who attended church services weekly donated an average of 3.3 percent of their income to nonprofits; those who attended monthly averaged 1.4 percent; and those who attended only once or twice a year averaged only 1 percent.

"Some 46 million American households give to charities but do not claim an income tax deduction."

- **Asked to give.** Whether or not individuals are asked to give has a tremendous impact on whether they donate to charitable organizations. Independent Sector found that of those households that were asked to give in 1995, 84.6 percent did so. On the other hand, only 44.1 percent of households not asked to contribute actually gave to charitable organizations. Likewise, 85.1 percent of individuals asked to volunteer actually did so, while only 20.7 percent of those not asked to contribute their time volunteered.
- **Demographics.** Several demographic factors influence the amount of income an individual donates to charity, regardless of income level. Specifically, retirees over the age of 65 give about 3.3 percent of their income to nonprofits. Those below the age of 45 give an average of about 1.6 percent of their income to charity. Those who are married or who have been married in the past donate about twice as much, on average, as a percentage of their income as do single individuals. And there is a strong relationship between volunteering and giving. The average amount donated to charitable causes by individuals who volunteer is more than twice as high as the average amount donated by individuals who do not volunteer.

Not All Charities Are Created Equal

Donating to different types of nonprofits varies widely across different categories of individuals. Upper-income individuals are more likely to give to the arts and humanities, environmental causes, and educational institutions. These same individuals are also more likely to itemize and, therefore, to claim a benefit from the current tax code.

Lower- and middle-income individuals, by contrast, are less likely to claim a charitable tax deduction under current law. They tend to give to religious congregations and human service groups. *Giving and Volunteering 1996* reports that in 1993, the average income for donors to the arts and humanities was

$56,535; the average for donors to environmental causes was $50,922; and the average for donors to educational institutions was $50,527. On the other end of the spectrum, the average income of donors to religious organizations was $40,923, and the average for donors to human service organizations was $47,099.

Put another way, an individual donor earning over $60,000 per year is seven times more likely to contribute to the arts and humanities than is a donor who earns less than $20,000 per year. Donations to educational institutions are 4.3 times more likely to come from wealthier individuals, and wealthier individuals are 3.7 times more likely to donate to environmental causes. On the other hand, wealthy donors (again, those earning more than $60,000 per year) are only 1.5 times more likely to donate to religious organizations and only 2.9 times more likely to donate to human service organizations.

These differences are significant when considering changes in the tax code. Independent Sector estimates that 65.3 percent of donors to the arts and humanities plan to itemize. Only 44.4 percent of donors to human services are itemizers, and only 38.1 percent of those who donate to religious organizations find it advantageous to itemize on their federal income tax returns.

Religious congregations enjoy the broadest base of support across all demographic groups. Therefore, it can be expected that instead of being hurt by the elimination of the charitable deduction, religious congregations will be helped significantly from the increased income generated by faster economic growth. In addition, since 92 percent of religious congregations across the nation are engaged in social activities and welfare programs, these charitable activities would enjoy a significant increase in funding as a result of the flat tax.

Human service / welfare organizations also could expect to benefit directly from the passage of a flat tax, but for two additional reasons.

First, individuals tend to see such donations as a basic obligation rather than as a discretionary action.

Second, the majority of donors to these activities are non-itemizers who would not be affected or dissuaded by the elimination of the charitable deduction, but who would be induced to give more thanks to their increased after-tax income.

The positive impact on welfare organizations would be amplified by what author Marvin Olasky calls *The Compassion Factor.* Stated simply, this is the understanding that Americans will become more involved in their communities, social institutions, and charitable organizations as government steps out of these areas (as would be the case with passage of a flat tax). As individuals become more involved, they develop more compassion for the less fortunate, and their financial and voluntary commitments increase.

The effect on other nonprofits, such as universities, art and theater companies, and environmental groups, which are most dependent on donations from the wealthy, is less clear. On the one hand, it is primarily the wealthy who take advantage of the charitable deduction. Donations may decrease for this reason. On the other hand, elimination of the capital gains and estate taxes would allow wealthy individuals to donate more money during their working years rather than setting the money aside in a bequest or foundation. Donations might increase for this reason.

In the long run, increased income as a result of lower taxes and increased economic growth will mean more donations for *all* nonprofits—the arts, environmental concerns, and universities included.

CONCLUSION

Any public policy must have a clearly defined goal. The task then becomes one of reaching that goal most efficiently and effectively.

In the case of the charitable contribution deduction, the goal is to encourage private giving to private organizations engaged in socially beneficial activities. It is unclear, however, whether the current tax system with a charitable contribution deduction is the most efficient and effective way to reach that goal. A better system might be a flat income tax with a single low rate and no deductions.

Historical evidence and economic analysis demonstrate that giving to nonprofit organizations will not decline with passage of the flat tax. In fact, donations likely will increase because of higher economic growth and increased personal income.

Bruce Bartlett, a Senior Fellow with the National Center for Policy Analysis, has served as Deputy Assistant Secretary for Economic Policy at the U.S. Treasury Department, a Senior Policy Analyst in the Office of Policy Development at the White House, and Executive Director and Deputy Director of the Joint Economic Committee. As a congressional staff member in the Washington office of New York Representative Jack Kemp, Mr. Bartlett helped draft the famous Kemp-Roth tax legislation. He writes a nationally syndicated column on economic policy, has authored four books, and has contributed more than 450 articles to such national publications as *The Wall Street Journal*, *The New York Times*, and *The Washington Post*. He received his B.A. from Rutgers University and his M.A. in American history from Georgetown University.

12

HOW THE FLAT TAX WILL HELP HOMEOWNERS

Bruce Bartlett
Senior Fellow
National Center for Policy Analysis

Elimination of the mortgage interest deduction is one of the most politically sensitive issues surrounding the flat tax. Those who own homes fear that loss of the deduction will raise their taxes and reduce the value of their homes. Their fears are stoked by the claims of special-interest groups that hope to maintain the status quo.

In reality, homeowners have nothing to fear from the adoption of a flat tax. Unbiased research shows that most homes will increase in value. And if the tax rate is 20 percent or lower, the vast majority of homeowners will pay less in taxes, not more.

Home ownership, not mortgage interest deductibility, is part of the American dream. Only a small number of taxpayers—just 27 percent—itemize their deductible expenses and benefit from the mortgage interest deduction. For nearly three-fourths of taxpayers, therefore, the deduction provides no benefit. Moreover, the few who do itemize are likely to be wealthy. Ninety percent of all the mortgage interest deducted is deducted by taxpayers with incomes over $50,000.

It is time to end the mortgage interest deduction and implement a flat tax. Homeowners and all other taxpayers will benefit.

THE TRUTH ABOUT THE MORTGAGE INTEREST DEDUCTION

In 1995, a Washington special-interest lobby, the National Association of Realtors, launched a major attack against one of the most popular issues in America: the flat tax. Its in-house newsletter even declared, "It's War!"—specifically, war against any tinkering with the mortgage interest deduction, a feature of the tax code since its inception in 1913 and one that would be abolished by a flat tax.

The realtors' lobby entered the fray armed with a traditional Washington weapon: a study. In this case, they paid DRI/McGraw-Hill, a private economic consulting firm, tens of thousands of dollars to analyze the flat tax. Not surprisingly, the study concluded that enacting a flat-rate income tax, such as that proposed by Representative Richard Armey (R–TX) and others, would cause home prices to fall by 15 percent, wiping out $1.7 trillion of homeowners' equity.

This cataclysmic outcome supposedly occurs because the mortgage interest deduction reduces the after-tax price of housing. DRI assumes that the value of this tax saving is fully reflected in the price of housing. Withdrawal of the mortgage interest deduction, therefore, reduces housing prices.

What DRI largely ignored in its analysis, however, is that tax rates would fall sharply under the Armey plan to a flat 17 percent rate for all taxpayers. Moreover, the Armey plan eliminates all interest from the tax base (payers could not deduct interest paid and savers would not be taxed on interest received), as well as the double taxation of corporate earnings. A balanced and objective study of the impact of a flat-rate tax on homeowners would have considered these changes. Doing so would suggest that, on balance, homeowners will benefit more from a flat tax than they might lose.

Recent Research. The conclusion reached in the DRI study is contradicted by recent research from some of the country's top economists. One of the first was J. D. Foster of the Tax Foundation. He found that the biggest "negative" effect would be a decline of 2 percent for houses in the $300,000 range. However, for many homeowners, the impact of the flat tax would be to raise housing prices. Foster found that the price of homes in the $100,000 range would rise by 12 percent, and the price of homes in the $200,000 range would rise by 3 percent. On balance, there would be little impact on housing prices overall.

A 1996 study by economist Jane Gravelle of the Congressional Research Service supported Foster's conclusions. She concluded that "the effects of the flat tax on housing prices are likely to be limited in the short run and very small in the long run." The principal reason is that the supply of housing, rather than prices, will absorb most of the impact of eliminating the mortgage interest deduction. Further, because taxes on interest income also would be eliminated, people would be likely to save more under a flat tax. Higher savings would tend to raise demand for housing in the long run.

The latest study to look at the impact of a flat tax on housing prices was published recently by the National Bureau of Economic Research. In "Apocalypse Now? Fundamental Tax Reform and Residential Housing Values," economists Donald Bruce and Douglas Holtz-Eakin of Syracuse University find modest effects on housing prices from elimination of the mortgage interest deduction. In fact, they find that a flat tax actually would raise housing prices by between 10 percent and 17 percent. They conclude that to the extent that fundamental tax reform is worthwhile, the effects on the housing industry should not stand in the way.

TAX RATES AND HOME PRICES

Historically, declining tax rates have been good for homeowners even though lower rates reduce the value of the deduction. For instance, when rates fall from 30 percent to 20 percent, tax savings drop by one-third. Thus, a $10,000 mortgage interest deduction would save a taxpayer in the 30 percent tax bracket $3,000 per year, but only $2,000 if the tax rate falls to 20 percent.

Therefore, if the DRI study was accurate, the rise in tax rates during the 1970s that resulted from bracket creep should have caused housing prices to rise. Conversely, the sharp reduction in tax rates during the 1980s should have caused housing prices to fall. In fact, the reverse happened, as James Poterba explained in a 1991 paper on "Housing Price Dynamics" for the Brookings Institution.

Table 11.1 looks at the inflation-adjusted price for median new homes and the average marginal tax rate. It shows that rising marginal tax rates did not raise the real price of new homes. The median new home price actually was less in 1982 than it was in 1973. By contrast, housing prices shot up when the Reagan tax cut became fully effective in 1983, and continued to rise even after the 1986 tax reform dropped tax rates further. These results cannot be explained by DRI's methodology.

> *"[A] flat tax will be good for housing. Elimination of taxes on interest received should cause all interest rates to fall....."*

One can argue, however, that housing prices were flat in the 1970s and rose in the 1980s despite the tax changes because changes in interest rates overwhelmed the tax effects. The new home mortgage rate rose from an average of 7.96 percent in 1973 to 15.14 percent in 1982. Rates fell thereafter, hit bottom in 1986 at 6.39 percent, and then rose to 8.8 percent by 1989.

It is certainly true that interest rates are an important factor in setting prices. The lower the interest rate, the more house one can afford on the same income. However, market interest rates to a large extent are set by tax rates. The higher the tax rate, the higher the interest rate (because lenders charge more to get the same after-tax return).

Table 12.1

Median New Home Price and Average Marginal Tax Rate

	Nominal Home Price	Real Home Price	Marginal Tax Rate
1973	$32,500	$73,198	29%
1974	35,900	72,819	30
1975	39,300	73,420	30
1976	44,200	77,680	31
1977	48,800	80,528	31
1978	55,700	85,429	32
1979	62,900	86,639	34
1980	64,600	78,398	35
1981	68,900	75,797	36
1982	69,300	71,813	33
1983	75,300	75,602	31
1984	79,900	76,901	30
1985	84,300	78,346	30
1986	92,000	83,942	30
1987	104,500	91,989	23
1988	112,500	95,097	23
1989	120,000	96,774	23

Note: Real home prices have been adjusted by the CPI.
Sources: U.S. Department of Housing and Urban Development; Bureau of Labor Statistics; Jane Gravelle, *The Economic Effects of Taxing Capital Income*, 1994.

Yet this demonstrates why a flat tax will be good for housing. Elimination of taxes on interest received should cause all interest rates to fall by approximately the spread between tax-free municipal bonds and comparable taxable securities, including mortgages. This means that if mortgage rates currently were at 8 percent, they should fall to 5.5 percent as soon as the flat tax takes effect. This is because a tax-free yield of 5.5 percent to mortgage lenders would be approximately the same as an 8 percent taxable yield.

As a result, new home buyers clearly will benefit. Current homeowners, meanwhile, can refinance to take advantage of substantially lower interest rates and come out ahead. In short, the impact of the flat tax on interest rates should more than offset elimination of the mortgage interest deduction.

It should be stressed that the decline in interest rates does not depend at all on any increase in the saving rate. It simply involves an equalization of taxable and tax-exempt yields. However, it is clear that elimination of all taxes on interest, coupled with ending the double taxation of dividends and capital gains, will increase saving. All other things being equal, this should cause interest rates to fall even more, further cushioning homeowners from the loss of mortgage interest deductibility.

The DRI study does assume a fall in interest rates, but it understates the amount because it compares municipal bond rates to 10-year Treasury bond rates. However, municipal bonds are much more risky than Treasury bonds (as holders of Orange County, California, bonds recently discovered), and Treasury bonds are also free of state taxes. Thus, the spread is much less than between municipals and comparable bonds, such as Baa corporate bonds.

Evidence from the States and Other Countries

Even without a decline in tax rates and interest rates, there is reason to believe that the loss of mortgage interest deductibility would have very little effect on prices or home ownership. International data, presented in Table 11.2, show that home ownership rates are not related to deductibility. Israel and Australia both have home ownership rates significantly higher than rates in the United States, yet do not allow mortgage interest deductibility. Home ownership rates in Canada and Japan are about the same—also without deductibility. By contrast, France and the Netherlands have much lower home ownership rates despite the deductibility of mortgage interest.

Table 12.2

Home Ownership Rates and Mortgage Interest Deductibility, 1992

	Ownership Rate	Interest Deductibility
Israel	73%	No
Australia	72	No
United Kingdom	68	Yes
United States	64	Yes
Canada	63	No
Japan	62	No
France	54	Yes
Netherlands	47	Yes
Germany	39	No

Source: International Housing Association, OECD.

The states also provide evidence, because 18 states either have no income tax or do not allow mortgage interest to be deducted from state taxes. Among the states with income taxes that do not allow mortgage interest to be deducted are Connecticut, Illinois, Indiana, Massachusetts, Michigan, New Jersey, Ohio, and Pennsylvania.

One would expect, at least according to DRI's analysis, that home ownership rates would be lower in states that do not provide any tax preference than in states that do provide such preference. Moreover, one would expect that the higher a state's tax rate, the higher the home ownership rate would be because the value of the deduction would be higher. In fact, the data show the opposite.

In 1993, the 18 states without an income tax or mortgage interest deductibility had an average home ownership rate of 64.8 percent—slightly higher than the national average of 64 percent. In fact, of the five states with the highest home ownership rates, three do not allow mortgage interest to be deducted from state taxes: Michigan (72.3 percent), Pennsylvania (72 percent), and West Virginia (73.3 percent).

At the same time, the states with the highest income tax rates and mortgage interest deductibility tend to have lower than average home ownership rates. The 12 states with the highest statutory tax rates (and the District of Columbia) have an average home ownership rate of just 61.8 percent. Of the six states with the lowest home ownership rates, four are among this group of 13. For example, California's top tax rate goes up to 11 percent—tied with Montana's for the highest in the nation—yet its home ownership rate is among the lowest at 56 percent. The District of Columbia, Hawaii, and New York also have high tax rates and home ownership rates well below average.

OTHER CONSIDERATIONS

It should be noted that 38 percent of homeowners currently have no existing mortgage on their homes, according to the Federal Reserve, and thus have no mortgage interest to deduct. Seventy-eight percent earn less than $50,000 annually, and 55 percent are over the age of 65 (see Table 11.3). Moreover, it is very likely that any flat tax passed by Congress would have a "transition rule" to allow homeowners who do not want to refinance to continue deducting interest for the life of their existing mortgages.

Nonetheless, let's look at a "worst-case" scenario. What about the possibility that the value of expensive homes—$300,000 and up—will decline by 2 percent under a flat tax?

First, any impact will be a one-time effect only. Once the value of the mortgage interest deduction that is built into the value of these homes is gone, housing prices should continue to rise at the same rate at which they otherwise would have risen.

Second, the supply of housing will absorb the loss of the mortgage interest deduction even under a worst-case scenario. That is, the supply of new housing will expand at a slower rate, while the prices of existing homes are unaffected. Realtors and homeowners, therefore, have nothing to fear.

Table 12.3

Characteristics of Homeowners With No Mortgage Debt

By Family Income	Percent
Less than $15,000	20%
15,000 – 24,999	26
25,000 – 49,999	32
50,000 – 74,999	12
75,000 – 99,999	5
100,000 or more	5
By Value of Home	
Less than $50,000	24%
50,000 – 99,999	38
100,000 or more	37
By Age of Homeowner	
18 – 34	7%
35 – 44	9
45 – 54	12
55 – 64	18
65 or older	55

Source: *Federal Reserve Bulletin*, April 1998.

Third, any modest loss of wealth will affect only those who had planned to sell their homes. But the vast majority of homeowners sell in order to buy another home. Since the loss of deductibility will affect all houses, people will be able to buy new houses for less. In other words, the actual cost of housing will not rise—lower prices on the homes people sell will be exactly offset by lower prices on those they buy.

Of course, insofar as housing prices do fall, the result will be of great benefit to first-time home buyers. Many of these people currently rent and thus receive no benefit from the mortgage interest deduction. Prospective home buyers also will benefit from the increase in after-tax income under a flat tax, and their increased ability to save for a down payment, once taxation of interest and the double taxation of dividends and capital gains are eliminated. Many studies have identified the lack of a sufficient down payment as a more important barrier to first-time home buyers than either housing prices or interest rates.

Table 12.4

Mortgage Interest Deduction, 1998

Income Class	Millions of Dollars	Percent
Below $10,000	$3	–
$10,000 – $20,000	128	0.3
$20,000 – $30,000	466	1.0
$30,000 – $40,000	1,238	2.6
$40,000 – $50,000	2,270	4.8
$50,000 – $75,000	7,667	16.3
$75,000 – $100,000	10,029	21.3
$100,00 – $200,000	15,739	33.5
$200,000 and over	9,438	20.1
Total	46,977	100.0

Source: U.S. Congress, Joint Committee on Taxation, *Estimates of Federal Tax Expenditures for Fiscal Years 1999–2003,* JCS-7-98.

Fourth, enactment of a flat tax unquestionably will increase growth and the value of stocks, bonds, and other investments. Professor Dale Jorgenson of Harvard estimates that national wealth would rise immediately by $1 trillion if a flat tax were implemented. And much of the increase in growth would come from eliminating the current tax bias in favor of investment in housing over other investments. A 1987 study by Professor Edwin Mills of Princeton estimated that equalizing the after-tax rate of return between housing and other capital would increase the stock of non-housing capital by 12 percent and increase real growth by 10 percent.

Finally, many tax reformers have criticized the mortgage interest deduction as unfair because the benefits rise with one's marginal tax rate, and thus one's income. As Table 11.4 indicates, 90 percent of all the mortgage interest that shows up in tax returns is deducted by taxpayers with incomes over $50,000. And since just 27 percent of taxpayers itemize, the mortgage interest deduction is of no value to at least 73 percent of taxpayers.

CONCLUSION

To be sure, the DRI study may make some valid points about the possible effects of a flat tax on the housing market, but it must be remembered that DRI was concerned only about the impact on housing because the National Association of Realtors paid $70,000 just for a study on housing. Thus, the study did not seriously consider the impact of a flat tax on economic growth, saving, or other factors that may overwhelm the impact on real estate.

Some flat tax supporters are tempted to modify the flat tax to accommodate the mortgage interest deduction. But the ultimate effect of such a concession would not be to enhance the political prospects for the flat tax, but to kill them completely. The reason is that once the purity of the flat tax is abrogated, we have embarked on a slippery slope that has no end. Once we make an exception for mortgage interest, there is no good argument for not keeping every other deduction as well.

Moreover, those who would retain the mortgage interest deduction seem not to realize how important its elimination is to the ultimate cause of fundamental tax reform. It distorts investment and slows economic growth. It is unfair because only a small number of taxpayers benefit. And it does little to stimulate home ownership.

Thus, as William T. Mathias recently concluded in an article in the University of Michigan *Journal of Law Reform*, the mortgage interest deduction is "inefficient, inequitable, and too costly." The realtors' self-serving study is flawed. Supporters of the flat tax should stick to their principles.

David R. Burton is a principal in the Argus Group, a law and government relations firm. He currently represents Americans for Fair Taxation, a citizens group dedicated to replacing the income tax and payroll taxes with a national sales tax. Mr. Burton has served as manager of the Tax Policy Center of the U.S. Chamber of Commerce, and as Vice President of Finance and General Counsel for New England Machinery, Inc., a small multinational manufacturer of packaging equipment and testing instrumentation based in Florida. He also was one of the principal lobbyists behind passage of the Taxpayer Bill of Rights. His articles on tax issues have appeared in publications ranging from *The Wall Street Journal* to *Tax Notes*. While at the Chamber of Commerce, he edited *The Journal of Economic Growth*. He is co-authoring a book on the national sales tax. Mr. Burton holds a J.D. degree from the University of Maryland.

13

THE NATIONAL SALES TAX ALTERNATIVE

David R. Burton
The Argus Group

Each year, Americans pay a steep price for the folly called the income tax. The current tax system forces Americans to accept a lower standard of living with lower wages and family income, destructively high compliance costs, an intrusive and unfair tax system that benefits lobbyists and special interests, industries that are less competitive, and a future with less hope and opportunity.

The United States needs a tax system that is more appropriate for a free society. This chapter briefly discusses the impact of the current tax system on individual Americans, how a national sales tax would work, and why a national sales tax would be an ideal way to raise revenues for the federal government.

HOW THE CURRENT TAX SYSTEM AFFECTS AMERICANS

A Lower Standard of Living. The income tax reduces economic growth by artificially holding down real wages. It makes U.S. goods and services less competitive in international markets. It impedes savings and capital formation, thereby slowing productivity, innovation, and growth. And it is biased against those who work hard to improve their standard of living. Graduated income taxes punish those who go to school to improve their skills, families with two breadwinners, and those who work at second and third jobs.

The message of the current income tax is that hard work, education, thrift, and entrepreneurial risk-taking should be punished. The harder you work, the more you improve your skills through education, the more you save, and the greater the risks you take, the higher your tax rate. Choose to save and you are double or triple taxed. You must pay for school with after-tax dollars, and your return from that education—a better-paying job—is taxed at steeply graduated rates.

The current federal income tax punishes the very behavior—work, saving, and investment—that is the most socially responsible and productive while disproportionately rewarding leisure and consumption. Hard work and thrift should not be singled out by the tax system for punitive treatment.

The economic object of overhauling the tax system is to correct this bias so that the tax system is neutral toward the decision to save and invest income or to consume it. Tax reform should reduce the bias against savings and work as much as is practical and impose an equal tax on labor income and capital income.

The current tax code's bias against savings and investment is staggering. If income is consumed, the benefits of consumption go untaxed. However, if income is saved or invested, the benefits of that saving—the earnings—are taxed again and again. Then, if income-producing assets, such as stocks or bonds, equipment, or real estate, are sold for more than it cost to purchase them originally, the capital gains are taxed yet

"The harder you work, the more you improve your skills through education, the more you save, and the greater the risks you take, the higher your tax rate."

again. Corporate income (including capital gains) is taxed at the corporate level and again when it is paid to shareholders as dividends.

An Intrusive and Unfair System. As hearings on Capitol Hill in 1997 showed, the Internal Revenue Service suffers from major administrative problems and, worse, does not adequately respect taxpayer rights. Some IRS employees are willing to do almost anything to improve their collection statistics. To protect against excessive enforcement, the law needs to be changed to enhance taxpayer rights.

> *"But the real problem is not the IRS. The real problem is the complexity of the current system."*

But the real problem is not the IRS. The real problem is the complexity of the current system, which is so monstrously complex that even professional tax preparers can only make educated guesses about how much tax their clients owe.

Each year, *Money* magazine surveys over 40 tax preparers and asks them to fill out a relatively simple middle-class tax return. Invariably, almost all of them get it "wrong." It is more accurate to say that they give "different" answers, because the tax system is so confusing that there really is no such thing as a "right" answer. A tax system that is this complex necessarily is administered in an arbitrary manner.

The IRS, of course, is in the business of raising money to pay for the federal government. It is not in the business of satisfying taxpayers or looking out for their interests. It must raise an estimated $1.7 trillion in FY 1999. To do this, the IRS employs over 100,000 people. In 1995 alone, it assessed more than 34 million civil penalties, required the issuance of over 1 billion information returns, and criminally prosecuted 3,400 people. Yet, according to recent IRS pronouncements, roughly $200 billion—about one-fifth of the income tax due—is not collected.

This "tax gap" is growing rapidly, both in absolute terms and as a percentage of national income. The system is beginning to collapse of its own weight.

High Compliance Costs. The nonpartisan Tax Foundation estimated in 1996 that we spend more than $150 billion complying with the income tax code each year. These costs are incorporated into the price of everything we buy. Adding the compliance costs of other federal taxes, this amounts to almost $850 for each man, woman, and child in America. That is $850 spent on needless, tax-related paperwork. We might as well burn it for all the good it does us. Americans would be better served if that money could be spent on education, housing, a family vacation, or whatever else they think would improve their quality of life.

We waste nearly 10 billion man-hours complying with the income tax system. Those hours could be used more productively, whether in designing new and better products, producing valuable goods and services, or spending more time with our families. Compliance costs are a much more substantial economic drag on small business than they are for larger businesses. Small businesses create most of the new jobs in this country. We should free entrepreneurs to develop, produce, and market their products and services instead of forcing them to spend time figuring out the complex tax code.

Reduced Global Competitiveness. The tax system makes U.S.-based firms and American workers less competitive in foreign as well as domestic markets. This happens primarily because the United States imposes the income tax and the payroll tax on domestic producers while foreign-produced goods do not bear these burdens.

HOW A NATIONAL SALES TAX WOULD WORK

Under a national sales tax, individuals no longer would need to file a tax return. The tax would be imposed on all retail purchases. All consumption would be taxed, including government purchases. In order to avoid double taxation, sales between businesses would not be taxed. Only businesses (including sole proprietors) would interact with the tax authorities, reporting their retail sales each month, and April 15 would become just another nice spring day for Americans.

Two Approaches

Two major national sales tax proposals have been introduced in Congress. Both are based on a comprehensive tax on goods and services that are consumed.

1. **The Tauzin Proposal.** Representative W. J. "Billy" Tauzin (R–LA) introduced legislation in the 105th Congress, with 19 co-sponsors, that would repeal the federal individual and corporate income tax, the estate and gift tax, and non-trust fund excise taxes. These taxes would be replaced by a low-rate national retail sales tax on consumption of goods and services. The proposal included a rebate that would reimburse households for the sales tax they pay on spending up to the federal poverty level. The Tauzin proposal would keep Social Security and Medicare taxes in place.
2. **The "FairTax" Proposal.** A Texas group, Americans for Fair Taxation (AFT), is promoting a sales tax plan called the FairTax. This plan, which is more detailed than the Tauzin proposal, likely will be introduced in both the House and the Senate on a bipartisan basis early in the 106th Congress. Although the FairTax is also a national sales tax on goods and services, it differs from the Tauzin proposal in a number of ways.

First, nothing would be withheld from a worker's paycheck. The FairTax would repeal Social Security and Medicare payroll taxes and the self-employment tax. This requires that the FairTax rate be higher than the Tauzin rate, probably by about eight percentage points.

Chart 13.1

Business Postcard for the National Retail Sales Tax

DRAFT **H.R. 2001 National Sales Tax Form**

Indicate the month to which this report relates: ____________, 200_

1	**Gross Sales**	Enter gross payments received from the sale of taxable property or services	$
2	**Sales Tax**	Enter 15 percent of the amount on line 1	$
3	**Administration Fee**	Multiply line 2 by 0.005	$
4	**Administration Fee**	Enter the larger of $200 of line 3 (may not exceed 20 percent of line 2)	$
5	**Credits (Optional)**	Enter total credits from line 13	$
6	**Total Credits and Fees**	Add line 4 and line 5	$
7	**Tax Due**	Subtract line 6 from line 2	$
		Remit the amount on line 7 to State X (if line 7 is negative, this amount will be refunded to you)	
8	**Bad Debt Credit**	Enter 15 percent of bad debts experienced (applies only to businesses electing the accrual method only)	$
9	**Business Use Credit**	Enter business use credit amount (applies only to businesses with property used for both business and personal purposes)	$
10	**Used Property Credit**	Enter used property credit due on sales of used property sold, if any, from line 16	$
11	**Insurance Proceeds Credit**	Enter 15 percent of insurance claims paid (for insurance companies only)	$
12	**Compliance Equipment Credit**	Enter 50 percent of the cost of qualified compliance equipment	$
13	**Total Credits**	Add lines 8 through 12	$
			$
14	**Sales of Appreciated Used Property**	Enter sum of sales tax paid by you when the used property was purchased	$
15	**Sales of Depreciated Used Property**	Enter sum of sales tax collected when used property was sold by you	$
16	**Total Used Property Credit**	Add line 14 and line 15	$

Source: Argus Group.

Second, the AFT plan would exempt used property from tax; the Tauzin proposal would not.

Third, the Tauzin proposal would repeal non-trust fund excise taxes, such as those on firearms, beer, wine, liquor, and tobacco. The FairTax would retain these taxes.

The Family Consumption Allowance

Under a national sales tax, no family would pay tax on the purchase of basic necessities. In effect, families would not be asked to support the government until they were able to support themselves. This is accomplished by providing a rebate to all families on their expenditures up to the federal poverty level. The rebate would be paid monthly, in advance. Under the FairTax plan, for example, the first $16,450 of consumption would not be taxed, which means a family of four would get a $315 check from the government each month.

No Loopholes

Under a national sales tax, all consumption would be taxed equally. Exempting goods such as food, housing, clothing, or medical care would shrink the tax base dramatically and raise the required rate on other goods and services; but if the aim is to get relief to low-income citizens, this is an ineffective way to do it. Exempting food would exempt both lobsters and hamburgers. Exempting clothing would exempt both $1,000 designer suits and T-shirts. Exempting housing would exempt apartments and townhouses, but it also would exempt mansions on 1,000-acre estates.

Such an approach would reinvigorate the special-interest lobbies to secure exemptions. It also would make the system more complex and raise compliance costs as businesses (and their lawyers and accountants) sought to comply with and take advantage of the system.

Is the National Sales Tax Like a State Sales Tax?

Although a national sales tax would be collected as sales taxes are collected in 45 states and the District of Columbia today, it differs from state sales taxes in four ways.

- **First,** various consumer goods or services would not be exempt.
- **Second,** business inputs would not be taxed; therefore, the sales tax would not be hidden or buried in the price of goods.
- **Third,** both national sales tax plans use a rebate mechanism to protect families from tax on basic necessities; state taxes do not.
- **Fourth,** both national sales taxes would be expressed on a tax-inclusive basis, with rates comparable to the income tax rate.

THE VIRTUES OF THE NATIONAL SALES TAX

1. **A national retail sales tax would improve the standard of living in America.**

   A sales tax is neutral in its treatment of saving and consumption. This means that it does not change the relative cost of saving and investment on the one hand and consumption on the other. Eliminating the double and triple taxation of saving by replacing the current income tax with a national retail sales tax reduces the tax burden on saving, thereby increasing the after-tax return to that capital. In turn, this would increase the amount a taxpayer saves and invests.

   Boston University economist Laurence Kotlikoff estimates that changing to a national sales tax will increase the saving rate dramatically. Real investment also will spike upward. Harvard University economist Dale Jorgenson forecasts that real investment would leap by 80 percent in the short term and remain about 20 percent higher than would be expected if the income tax were still in place. As a direct result of this dramatic increase in real investment, capital stock (machinery, equipment, factories, and buildings) will increase.

Virtually all economic studies predict a much healthier economy if the current tax system is replaced with a national sales tax. Typical estimates are that the economy will be 10 percent to 14 percent larger than it would be under the current income tax in the first ten years. Consumption, savings, investment, and real wages will grow substantially. An economy this healthy will mean that everyone who wants a job can get one. It will mean better-paying jobs and greater opportunities for advancement. Family budgets will improve. The federal budget also will improve, because a strong economy causes tax revenues to go up and welfare spending to decline.

The economic growth forecast by most computer-based macroeconomic models is primarily a function of greater productivity that results from increased capital investment. Simply put, workers will be able to produce more because they will have more capital (plant, machinery, and equipment) with which to work.

The models typically do not assume that people will choose to work more. Nor do they take into account the positive impact of significantly increased capital inflow from abroad that a national sales tax likely will precipitate. The models tend to attach little importance to the microeconomic efficiencies that would be generated by eliminating tax loopholes so that resources are allocated based on economic rather than tax considerations. Finally, they do not account for productivity gains from large reductions in private compliance costs. Thus, there is strong reason to believe that a national retail sales tax will cause even more significant economic growth than Jorgenson, Kotlikoff, or other macroeconomic modelers now predict.

Investment is important to all Americans. The most important cause of higher real wages is a higher level of capital investment per worker. A worker or farmer will be more productive if he or she has more and better machinery and equipment with which to work, particularly if that new equipment incorporates the latest technological innovations.

Moreover, higher productivity leads to higher real wages. An American farmer does not live better than his counterpart in Bangladesh because he works more hours; he lives better because he has more capital to use. It is impossible, on a sustained basis, for an employer to pay workers higher wages than their productivity justifies, because employers that did so would soon go out of business.

The combination of a highly attractive tax system, stable political and legal institutions, a well-educated work force, good infrastructure, and a large domestic market will make American-based operations highly attractive. To paraphrase Ross Perot's memorable expression, the giant sucking sound you hear will be U.S. businesses sucking up investment capital from around the world to finance new plants and create more jobs here at home. American workers will build these plants. Most of the equipment installed in these plants will be American. Americans will be employed in these plants to produce goods for domestic as well as foreign markets. And because investment in U.S. plants would be more attractive than under current law, U.S. firms will not need to move their plants overseas to remain competitive.

The median household income in 1995 was $40,611. Under current policies, this will not double in real, inflation-adjusted terms until 2031. But if the federal government adopts economic policies that increase growth to historic levels, the typical family's income will double in real terms by 2014, and will virtually quadruple by 2031. The battle for tax reform is nothing less than the battle to improve the standard of living of typical American families.

2. **A national sales tax would be visible and would convey the true cost of government.**

   Each and every purchase consumers make would remind them of the cost of government. Moreover, taxes no longer would be hidden from view. This is in contrast to many of today's taxes—such as the corporate income tax and the employer's share of payroll taxes—that take people's money surreptitiously.

3. **A national sales tax would be fairer.**

   A national sales tax is fairer than the current income tax because it taxes people on the basis of what they use for their own enjoyment over and above the basic necessities of life, rather than what they produce or earn. It does not punish hard work, education, or thrift. It does not contain special exemptions, exclusions, or credits for the well-to-do or the politically powerful, but instead treats people equally. It would promote upward mobility by allowing people to work, save, or invest to improve their financial standing without being punished by the tax system. It is fair because it allows people to understand the tax system and their tax burden.

4. **A national sales tax would reduce compliance costs.**

   A national sales tax is a simple tax, and one that almost anyone can understand. It would radically reduce the compliance burden. Indeed, under a national sales tax, most Americans would never need to deal with the federal tax authorities. Taxes would not be withheld from employees' paychecks, and individuals who were not in business would not file returns.

For businesses, the only question would be, "How much did I sell to my consumers?" No more complex depreciation rules; no alternative minimum tax; no army of paid experts to help them comply with complex pension and deferred compensation rules; no complex rules regarding taxable and non-taxable employee benefits; no uniform capitalization rules regarding inventory; no complex international tax rules; no capital gains, estate, and gift taxes that force many families to sell the family business or farm to pay them—the list could go on.

5. **A national sales tax would reduce tax evasion.**

   It is well-established in academic literature that the most important factor leading to tax evasion is the marginal tax rate. The higher the marginal tax rate, the greater the benefit from tax evasion and the more likely it is that people will evade the tax system. A national sales tax dramatically reduces marginal tax rates.

   Another major factor is the risk of detection and punishment. The national sales tax would reduce the number of filers by over 90 percent. The tax authorities would be freer to focus audit and investigation efforts on those who try to evade paying taxes. As the risk of detection increases, the probable cost of evasion increases, and tax evasion would decline.

6. **A national sales tax would exempt exports and tax imports.**

   A national sales tax would not tax exports. Imported goods would be taxed when they are sold at retail stores in the United States, just as domestically produced goods would be taxed. Exports would not be subject to the tax since they would not be sold at retail stores in America.

COMPARING A FLAT TAX AND A NATIONAL SALES TAX

On the two most important issues of tax policy—what should be taxed and what rate structure will be imposed—flat tax proponents and national sales tax proponents are largely in agreement. This is because both the national sales tax and the flat tax are single-rate consumption-based taxes.

Both the flat tax and the sales tax have a single flat rate. Both proposals exempt a certain amount of annual income or consumption from the tax. The flat tax uses an allowance based on family size, while the sales tax uses a rebate mechanism. Both taxes are neutral toward savings and investment. Neither punishes hard work or thrift by imposing graduated tax rates. Both proposals would radically reduce compliance costs. Both would significantly increase economic growth and dramatically improve the standard of living in the United States. And both proposals are fairer than the current tax system.

Under a national sales tax, consumption is taxed directly and in an obvious way. Under the flat tax, it is less obvious. The overall flat tax base is equal to output less investment (since investment expenses may be deducted in their entirety in the year they are incurred). What remains is consumption. Output is taxed in two separate places. Labor output is taxed at the individual level; capital output is taxed at the business level.

Proponents of the flat tax and the national sales tax differ on what is the best way to collect a single-rate consumption-based tax. Naturally, there can be legitimate differences of opinion about which proposal is most likely to achieve the most public support. But in the final analysis, those who support a flat tax and those who advocate a sales tax share many important values and aspirations in working for tax reform.

CONCLUSION

Proponents of the national sales tax believe it offers the best method of collecting the revenues the federal government needs to operate. Replacing the current system with a national sales tax also would enhance the standard of living of all Americans and is much more in keeping with the values of a free society than is the current income tax.

Grover G. Norquist is President of Americans for Tax Reform, a coalition of taxpayer groups, individuals, and businesses opposed to higher federal and state taxes. Previously, he served on the National Commission on Restructuring the Internal Revenue Service and was the Executive Director of the National Taxpayers Union. Mr. Norquist authors the monthly column "Politics" for the *American Spectator.* He holds an M.B.A. degree and a B.A. in economics from Harvard University.

14

HOW A SUPERMAJORITY PROTECTS FUTURE GENERATIONS

Grover G. Norquist
President, Americans for Tax Reform

Taxpayers correctly fear that the benefits of tax reform will be undermined if future politicians increase tax rates or create new taxes. Whether we adopt a flat tax or a national retail sales tax, there are three key principles that Congress must consider to ensure real long-term reform of the tax system:

1. Income or consumption expenditures must be taxed only once.
2. Income or consumption must be taxed at one single low rate.
3. A constitutional amendment requiring a two-thirds vote in Congress to raise taxes or enact new taxes is imperative.

This last point is crucial. Should Congress enact a low single-rate tax *without a supermajority amendment*, pro-spending forces could push each year for a "small" tax increase to do "good things." The career politicians who believe in big government will try to overcome taxpayer objections by selecting emotional causes. They likely will claim, for instance, that a 1 percent increase in the tax rate would be for the good of children or to cure cancer. If they succeeded, after five years, a 17 percent flat tax might be a 21 percent flat tax. And ten years after that, the rate might be 30 percent.

This is not a theoretical concern. We saw something similar happen after the 1986 Tax Reform Act that created two rates, one at 15 percent and another at 28 percent. First President Bush and then President Clinton enacted tax hikes on top of President Reagan's reform. A two-thirds supermajority would have stopped both tax hikes. It is much harder to get 67 votes in the Senate and 290 votes in the House than it is to muscle through a tax increase by a bare majority. As a result, a supermajority requirement to raise taxes will make it easier to protect taxpayers.

Advocates of a retail sales tax also need to demand a supermajority amendment to prevent the re-emergence of the federal income tax. Repealing the Sixteenth Amendment (the one that allowed an income tax) will not be enough. The Supreme Court might allow Congress to re-impose such a tax unless it were specifically prohibited, and even then, some lawyerly debate might offer ways around any constitutional prohibition. Only the firewall of a two-thirds supermajority vote to raise taxes could ensure that the income tax is not reimposed on top of a national sales tax. Thus, all advocates of real reform have a strong interest in supporting a supermajority constitutional amendment.

> *"Should Congress enact a low single-rate tax* without a supermajority amendment, *pro-spending forces could push each year for a 'small' tax increase to do 'good things.'... If they succeeded, after five years, a 17 percent flat tax might be a 21 percent flat tax. And ten years after that, the rate might be 30 percent."*

Congresses historically have been incapable of restraining their taxing and spending habits. The evidence is compelling. When faced with a choice of trimming the federal budget or squeezing the family budget, politicians almost always have chosen to raise taxes. Even if tax reform never happens, a supermajority should be implemented. Critics argue that a supermajority is untested, ineffective, and unconstitutional; but consider the following evidence:

Table 14.1

The Supermajority in the States

	Requirement	Enacted	Passed By	Applies to
Arizona	2/3 elected	1992	Initiative	All taxes
Arkansas	3/4 elected	1934	Referendum	All taxes
California	2/3 elected	1979	Initiative	All taxes
Colorado	2/3 elected	1992	Initiative	All taxes
Delaware	2/3 elected	1992	Initiative	All taxes
Florida*	3/5 elected	1980	Referendum	Corporate income tax
	2/3 voters	1996	Initiative	All taxes
Louisiana	2/3 elected	1966	Referendum	All taxes
Mississippi	3/5 elected	1890, 1970	Referendum (1970)	All taxes
Missouri	2/3 elected	1996	Referendum	All taxes
Nevada	2/3 elected	1996	Initiative	All taxes
Oklahoma	3/4 elected	1992	Initiative	All taxes
Oregon	3/5 elected	1996	Initiative	All taxes
South Dakota	2/3 elected	1978	Initiative	All taxes
Washington	2/3 elected	1993	Initiative	All taxes

Note: *Florida law mandates that state revenues be limited to those collected in the prior fiscal year, plus an adjustment for growth. State revenue levels for any fiscal year may be increased by a two-thirds vote of the membership of each house in the legislature on a bill that contains no other subject and sets forth the dollar amount by which the state revenues allowed will be increased. Florida Constitution Article VII, Section 19(e).

1. **Supermajority requirements exist at the state level.**
   Supermajorities have a successful track record. Many states have supermajority tax limitation laws. Indeed, over one-third of Americans live in states that have enacted supermajority constitutional tax limitations. In most of these states, the supermajority requirement grew out of the tax revolt movement and the use of the ballot initiative.

   These states offer a successful model for the federal government's budget and tax reform efforts. As seen in Table 14.1, a two-thirds vote is required to raise taxes in most of the states that require a supermajority.

2. **Supermajorities work.**
   Many states have enacted supermajorities so recently that there is not enough evidence to draw meaningful conclusions. As seen in the table, however, several have had supermajorities for quite some time. Comparing the fiscal performance of these states to that of states without the provision shows that supermajorities work. Between 1980 and 1992, for instance, per capita tax revenues climbed by 121 percent in non-supermajority states. In states with this protection, by contrast, revenues grew by 102 percent.

   > *"The supermajority forces them to reduce wasteful spending before resorting to tax increases, and it makes them more accountable to taxpayers."*

   In supermajority states, lawmakers are required to reach a broad consensus before enacting a tax increase. The supermajority forces them to reduce wasteful spending before resorting to tax increases, and it makes them more accountable to taxpayers. Supermajority requirements not only lead to lower tax burdens at the state level, but also result in reduced overall state government spending. Looking again at the 1980 to 1992 period, states with supermajorities increased spending at a slower rate than states without a supermajority. The difference was not very large, but every penny counts.

This evidence probably explains why so many states have enacted supermajorities in the 1990s. Because they slow the growth of government and keep tax burdens under control, supermajorities boost economic growth by leaving more resources in the productive sector of the economy. Once again, the evidence from the 1980s shows the benefit of tax limitation. The economies of supermajority states grew faster, thereby creating more jobs, than did those of non-supermajority states. There is every reason to believe similar economic benefits will materialize if the federal government adopts a two-thirds requirement before taxes can be increased.

3. **A supermajority requirement is consistent with the Constitution.**

Not only is a supermajority requirement necessary for the future economic health of the nation, but it is consistent with existing constitutional supermajority voting requirements. In ten instances, the Constitution mandates supermajority voting requirements. Each of these requirements reflects thoughtful deliberation by the Framers of the Constitution. Each also serves a purpose and illustrates the capacity of the Constitution's architects to impose such requirements on Congress when they deemed it necessary or useful.

When it was appropriate in the political environment of the 1780s to prescribe a specific numerical voting requirement, the Constitution supplied one (see Table 14.2). True, the Framers did not include a supermajority for tax increases, but remember that there was no income tax back then, and the federal government was only a fraction of the size it is today. Had the Founders known that future politicians would allow runaway deficits and massive government in the absence of a compelling national emergency, they probably would have required a supermajority for tax increases as well. Politicians in Washington, D.C., cannot be trusted to protect the pocketbooks of Americans without a requirement that there be broad support for any tax increase.

There is nothing in the U.S. Constitution that requires legislation to be passed by a bare majority of Congress. The Presentment Clause in Article I, Section 7, simply states that "Every Bill which shall have passed the House of Representatives and the Senate, shall, before it becomes a Law, be presented to the President of the United States...." The Presentment Clause does not specify a proportion necessary for passage. Consequently, arguments that the Tax Limitation Amendment violates the Constitution by mandating a requirement that legislation be passed by any ratio other than a majority of a quorum vote are without merit. From the early days of the Republic to the present, supermajority voting requirements have been deemed constitutional.

The Framers' decision not to impose even more constitutional supermajority requirements than those listed in the table does not mean that they opposed the concept. It simply means that, at the time of ratification, they did not see a need for other such requirements.

However, they did recognize that circumstances change and that the Constitution would need to be flexible enough to change with the passage of time. Consequently, they provided a mechanism to amend the Constitution that itself includes two supermajority voting requirements—approval by two-thirds of Congress to adopt the proposed

Table 14.2

Supermajority Requirements in the U.S. Constitution

Article I, Section 3, Clause 6	Conviction in impeachment trials
Article I, Section 5, Clause 2	Expulsion of a Member of Congress
Article I, Section 7, Clause 2	Override a presidential veto
Article II, Section 1, Clause 3	Quorum of two-thirds of the states to elect the President
Article II, Section 2, Clause 2	Consent to a treaty
Article V	Proposing constitutional amendments
Article VII	State ratification of the original Constitution (9 out of 13 states)
Amendment XII	Quorum of two-thirds of the states to elect the President and Vice President
Amendment XIV	To remove disability of those who have engaged in insurrection
Amendment XXV, Section 4	Presidential disability

amendment, and then approval by three-fourths of the states for ratification.

Finally, a supermajority requirement for increasing the tax burden is not unprecedented. The Sixteenth Amendment to the Constitution, which provides for the income tax, had to be approved by a vote of two-thirds of Congress and three-fourths of the states. It is only logical that we should extend this protection to tax increases that already greatly exceed the small burden first imposed in 1913.

The method for deciding fundamental issues facing the U.S. government was one of the most important topics addressed by the Founders during the drafting of the U.S. Constitution. In the Federalist Papers, Alexander Hamilton, James Madison, and John Jay argued that rule by a simple majority vote was tantamount to mob rule. They argued that the Constitution was to prevent transitory passions from determining the outcome of crucial decisions for the country.

Madison argued in Federalist No. 51 that the greatest threat to liberty in a republic came from unrestrained majority rule. Hamilton argued in Federalist No. 73 for the checking of simple majorities through the use of the President's veto power. Hamilton recognized that two-thirds majorities to override a veto might prevent the enactment of good laws, but responded that any injury inflicted by defeating a few good laws would be compensated by the advantage of preventing a number of bad laws. Hamilton also argued in Federalist No. 22 that to prevent tax abuse, direct taxes required explicit constitutional constraints.

The Founders believed that fundamental decisions should be made by special majorities of at least two-thirds of the legislature. They pointed specifically to such areas as the ratification of treaties and constitutional amendments. They felt that even in the deliberative bodies, a narrow majority of Congress might easily be put together to force the quick adoption of a decision that would have lasting and harmful consequences. The Framers of the Constitution understood that truly good ideas would receive—and should receive—the backing of a two-thirds supermajority.

Implementing a Supermajority. Making it more difficult to raise taxes is a good idea regardless of what else is happening. But if lawmakers are making important reforms, such as a flat tax or a balanced budget amendment, making it harder to raise taxes is a great idea. The simplest, fairest, and safest way to implement a supermajority is to adopt a tax limitation amendment to the Constitution. The language would be very straightforward, requiring that all increases in the tax burden be subject to a supermajority vote by both houses of Congress.

The other alternative is to enact a law requiring a supermajority. But this would be less secure, since laws can be eliminated or modified by future politicians, and it is safe to assume that a Congress that wanted to go on a spending spree would have few qualms about repealing any supermajority that made it harder to raise taxes.

This means that tax reform could be undermined by a gradual increase in tax rates. Unfortunately, history shows that politicians are able to take reasonable laws and make them oppressive. The first income tax, for instance, had a top rate of only 7 percent, and it cannot be doubted that the lawmakers who approved that tax would have voted "no" if they knew how their simple tax code would degenerate into the monstrosity we have today.

Failure to implement a constitutional supermajority also means there would be no way to prevent politicians from simply raising taxes to meet the requirements of any balanced budget law. Simply stated, the best way to prevent your representatives in Washington from raising taxes is to adopt a Tax Limitation Amendment with its requirement of an affirmative supermajority vote of both houses of Congress for any increase in the tax burden.

The Tax Limitation Amendment is good policy. In those states that require legislative supermajorities to increase the tax burden, the method has proved to be an effective tool for lowering both tax burdens and government spending. The Tax Limitation Amendment is a sound modification of the Constitution. There already are numerous supermajority voting requirements mandated by the Constitution. The United States was founded in part on the basis of freedom from oppressive taxes—clearly a concept lost on lawmakers who tax to finance runaway spending.

4. **The supermajority counters special-interest lobbying power.**

   The flat tax is a good idea even if a supermajority is not included. After all, it would give us more freedom and prosperity while it lasted. If possible, however, the supermajority should be added to protect taxpayers in the future. If politicians ten years from now want to increase spending for pet projects, Congress should be compelled to reduce spending elsewhere to keep the budget in balance. And data from states that now have some form of tax increase supermajority show that the requirement *does* force lawmakers to set priorities.

   For more than 50 years, concentrated and vocal interest groups have been able to secure costly benefits for themselves that are paid for by the widely scattered majority of taxpayers. Due to its far-flung nature, the taxpaying majority is usually ineffective in stopping federal government largess.

   Consider the example of a 1 percent increase in a flat tax. Such a change would raise about $40 billion in new tax revenue. Interest groups would have a big incentive to lobby and create coalitions in order to get their hands on a share of the loot. After all, success could mean tens of thousands of dollars for each member of the group.

   But what about taxpayers? They would be against the rate increase, it is true, but their tax bills would increase by an average of only $300 to $350. That might be enough to instigate a phone call or a letter to their representatives in

Congress. A few might even attend a town hall meeting to register their displeasure. This is a minor effort, though, particularly when compared to the highly organized campaign that would be waged by the interest groups.

This is why a constitutional amendment mandating a two-thirds affirmative vote of Congress to increase taxes will improve the legislative process. It will offset the lobbying ability of special interests. Groups seeking to pick taxpayers' pockets will have to persuade a larger group of legislators that they need the handout.

5. **A supermajority amendment is popular.**

Taxpayer protection is good policy and good politics. In a recent survey conducted by *the polling company*™,

- **75 percent** of registered voters responded that they would be more likely to vote to re-elect their current Member of Congress if he or she voted for a two-thirds supermajority.
- **73 percent** of registered voters support a two-thirds supermajority vote requirement to make it difficult for Congress to raise taxes.
- **72 percent** believe there is no need for Congress to raise taxes.
- **79 percent** believe it should be more difficult to raise taxes than to cut spending.
- **72 percent** believe that a two-thirds supermajority would end tax increases passed with only one-party support.
- **70 percent** believe that a two-thirds supermajority requirement would reduce the size of government.
- **70 percent** support a constitutional amendment to require a two-thirds supermajority.

- **78 percent** would feel more confident of their state taxes if they learned their state had a two-thirds supermajority (as they have, for example, in California).
- **68 percent** would be more likely to support a complete replacement of the current tax system if it included a two-thirds supermajority.

Lawmakers have responded to this strong support. Senator Jon Kyl (R–AZ) and Representatives Joe Barton (R–TX), John Shadegg (R–AZ), Ralph Hall (D–TX), and Virgil Goode (D–VA) have introduced in the U.S. Congress a Tax Limitation Amendment to the Constitution of the United States, requiring a two-thirds supermajority for any new tax or increase in existing taxes. The main provision states that "[a]ny bill to levy a new tax or increase the rate or base of any tax may pass only by a two-thirds majority of the whole number of each House of Congress."

Perhaps more significantly, this amendment is supported strongly by flat tax advocates *and* sales tax proponents. All tax reformers understand that a supermajority is the best way to ensure that reform is not just a short-term victory.

CONCLUSION

Passing the supermajority requirement is an important element of successful tax reform. Constitutional tax limitations keep government spending under control and protect taxpayers from ever-increasing tax rates. With its current commitment to keep the budget balanced, the government will be forced to set spending levels in accordance with actual revenues. Over time, the level of government spending will fall to its optimal level. The result: increased growth in both personal incomes and government revenue as the economy expands.

Americans support moving to a single-rate tax that taxes income only one time. Scrapping the current tax code and implementing a simple and fair system like the flat tax will create more prosperity and freedom—but only if the rate is kept low. Imposing the constitutional requirement for a two-thirds supermajority to raise taxes would protect Americans from such tax hikes and ensure real tax freedom in the future.

15

CONCLUSION

Daniel J. Mitchell
McKenna Senior Fellow in Economic Policy
The Heritage Foundation

WHY LAWMAKERS MUST BE BOLD

Fixing the tax code will not be easy. The mess we have today is a testament to the influence of special-interest politics, and a flat tax will have to overcome powerful groups that want to preserve the status quo. Some battles are worth fighting, however, even when the odds are steep.

Recall the dire shape our economy was in during the late 1970s. Inflation was climbing, unemployment was rising, and there was a widespread perception that America was facing a permanent era of "stagflation" and economic decline. Yet a small band of courageous lawmakers, led by Jack Kemp (R–NY) in the House and William Roth (R–DE) in the Senate, realized that our problems were the fault of misguided government policies. These "supply-siders" pointed out that 70 percent tax rates were stifling initiative and encouraging taxpayers to hide their income. They proposed sweeping, across-the-board tax rate reductions.

At first, their ideas were ignored. Then, as they slowly picked up steam, they were attacked. Eventually, this "risky" idea was endorsed by a former governor from California, who rode the issue all the way to the White House.

The rest, as they say, is history. The economy boomed, incomes rose, and jobs were created at a record pace. Inflation and interest rates fell dramatically, and America became an engine of prosperity.

The time has come for courageous leaders today to follow the path blazed by Representative Kemp and Senator Roth. Our tax code is unfair. It is riddled with social engineering. The system is corrupt, and it undermines opportunity for those most in need. The American people understand that the tax code is irretrievably broken, and they will be receptive to bold and visionary leadership.

"This incremental strategy is appealing, but it may not be realistic. For one thing, the one-step-at-a-time approach is what produced the current tax code."

The time is right for the flat tax.

A question often asked, however, is whether implementing a flat tax requires too much change at one time. Yes, it does create the ideal system, skeptics admit, but why not try to appease the special interests by fixing the tax code's myriad problems in a step-by-step fashion? Reduce tax rates one year, repeal the death tax the following year, end double taxation of dividends the year after that, and keep the process going until everything wrong with the current system is fixed and a flat tax is achieved.

This incremental strategy is appealing, but it may not be realistic. For one thing, the one-step-at-a-time approach is what produced the current tax code. Yes, positive changes are implemented every so often, but it is just as likely that politicians in any given year will move us even further in the wrong direction. Even when lawmakers move in the right direction, they may do so in a bizarre way.

Consider the 1997 tax cut. This legislation had many positive features, including the fact that it was the first tax reduction in 16 years. Yet, because Congress and the White House engaged in so much horse-trading, they wound up making everything more complex. The bill created more than 250 new sections in the tax code and amended more than 800 others.

For this reason, lawmakers should reject the piecemeal approach and adopt the flat tax. It is true that some special-interest groups will oppose a flat tax. It is also true that some politicians will instinctively resist reform because it will take away so much of their power and make it harder for them to raise campaign contributions. But the flat tax also offers certain political advantages:

- **Coalition support.** The flat tax solves all of the tax code's problems at once. People who are angry about the capital gains tax can join forces with others who are upset about the code's complexity. Taxpayers fed up with high rates can find common ground with business owners frustrated with depreciation and the alternative minimum tax. Farmers angry about the death tax can work with savers upset about double taxation. A serious campaign to implement the flat tax could count on a wide-ranging base of support. In other words, when it comes to winning, the whole is greater than the sum of its parts.

> *"The flat tax solves all of the tax code's problems at once."*

- **Political popularity.** In the real world, polls matter. The flat tax is not a guaranteed winner, but it consistently generates support from 50 percent to 65 percent of voters. This popularity is driven largely by the public's desire to have a simple and fair tax system that gets the IRS out of their lives. Ironically, many of the component parts of the flat tax, such as capital gains tax repeal and the abolition of loopholes, are not very popular, especially if considered as free-standing pieces of legislation. Once again, the whole is greater than the sum of its parts.

- **Freedom and civil liberties.** Supporters of the flat tax can argue that sweeping reform means substantially expanding civil liberties and creating a tax code based on widely shared moral values. This means that a flat tax will attract voters who may not care about the overall tax burden and may not understand how the current system undermines prosperity. They may want all taxpayers to be treated equally, or they may want to defang the IRS, or they may want simplicity and transparency. Whatever their goal, these citizens will add their voices to those who support tax reform for more traditional (and often self-interested) reasons.

"The only hope for victory is to repeal the entire code and start over."

Trying to fix this monstrosity one piece at a time is probably an impossible task. For every step forward, there will be two steps backward. The only hope for victory is to repeal the entire code and start over. Have lawmakers sit down with a blank piece of paper and draw up a tax code that fulfills the promise of equality before the law. Let them imagine the kind of world they want for their children and grandchildren.

Appealing to the best in everyone is the right way to achieve true tax reform. A flat tax is possible. All it takes is a commitment to do the right thing.

GLOSSARY

Alternative minimum tax (AMT)—A provision in the tax code that requires certain individuals and businesses to calculate their taxes two ways and pay the government the larger of the two amounts. In general, the AMT takes effect when deductions are "too large" relative to income. This means that the tax often applies during economic downturns, when income falls but expenses remain relatively unchanged.

Armey–Shelby flat tax—The best-known of the flat tax plans introduced in Congress. It is a pure approach, containing no loopholes except for a generous allowance based on family size.

Average tax rate—The overall share of income taken by the government. A taxpayer with $50,000 of income who pays $10,000 in taxes faces an average tax rate of 20 percent.

Capital gains tax—A tax that applies when an asset is sold for more than its original purchase price. The tax applies to the "gain" that has occurred, but the taxpayer is not allowed to adjust for inflation.

Charitable contributions deduction—A provision in the current tax code that allows taxpayers to deduct contributions made to charities which have been granted special status by the IRS.

Consumption tax—A tax system often associated with taxes collected at the cash register, but any system that does not double-tax savings and investments is a consumption tax.

The flat tax and the "consumed-income" tax (basically an unlimited individual retirement account) are consumption-based income taxes.

Consumption tax base—A tax system that treats all income equally. All income is taxed, but only once (though not necessarily at the same rate). In the case of the income tax, this means that there are no deductions, and income that is exempt (such as fringe benefits) is subject to the tax. Conversely, it also means that no income is taxed more than once, thus precluding capital gains or estate taxes.

Death tax—A form of taxation under which the assets of taxpayers who accumulate "too much" savings during their lifetime are subject to a tax upon death. The rate for this tax reaches 55 percent under the current code.

Deductions—Amounts or types of income that can be excluded from taxable income. In addition to personal exemptions, taxpayers can take either a standard deduction or itemized deductions, such as home mortgage interest and charitable contributions.

Depreciation—Provision by which, for example, a business that invests $1 million buying a new machine is not allowed to fully deduct that cost when calculating its taxable income. Instead, it may deduct only a portion of the cost each year. Depreciation is complex, and it increases the tax burden on investment.

Double taxation—Form of taxation under which any dollar of income is subject to more than one level of tax. The classic example is income that is taxed at the corporate level and then taxed again as dividend income when received by the shareholder. With capital gains taxes and estate taxes, it is possible for a single dollar of income to be taxed four times.

Estate tax—*See* death tax.

Flat tax—A single-rate tax system. A flat tax and sales tax are almost identical in that a flat tax imposes one layer of tax when income is earned and a sales tax imposes one layer of tax when income is spent. In either case, all income is taxed, but only once and presumably at a very low rate. *See* Armey–Shelby flat tax.

Hall–Rabushka—Robert Hall and Alvin Rabushka, the two economists at Stanford University who developed the simple and pure flat tax model.

Itemized deductions—Write-offs for such expenses as charitable contributions, home mortgage interest, and state and local income and property taxes. A taxpayer may not use both itemized deductions and the standard deduction. Under the current system, more than 70 percent of taxpayers use the standard deduction.

Marginal tax rate—The amount of additional earnings taken by government. The taxpayer with $50,000 of income may face a 28 percent tax rate on the next dollar of income earned, even though the average tax rate for this taxpayer's income is 20 percent. The marginal tax rate affects incentives to offer additional labor and/or capital to the economy.

Marriage penalty—The many provisions in the tax code that cause married couples to pay more in taxes than they would pay if they were single and living together. Graduated tax rates account for the largest share of the marriage penalty.

Mortgage interest deduction—A provision which allows taxpayers who itemize to deduct from their income each year the money they pay in mortgage interest.

National sales tax—A nationwide tax imposed on final retail sales of goods and services to the consumer. This tax presumably would apply to all goods and services and usually is discussed in conjunction with total repeal of the income tax.

Neutrality—A concept which argues that the tax system should not affect economic decisions. A neutral tax system, for instance, would not encourage either savings or consumption. Nor would it bias choices among types of consumption or types of savings.

Personal exemption—An amount of income which the taxpayer is allowed to shield from tax. The current tax code, as well as most proposed reforms, grants exemptions for each additional dependent member of a household. This "zero-bracket" amount would increase with family size.

Preferential treatment—Treatment which occurs if certain incomes or activities receive favoritism. In the case of a sales tax, for instance, a narrow base would mean that major items like food, shelter, clothing, and health care are not subject to the tax. Assuming that policymakers intend to collect a given amount of tax revenue, allowing preferential treatment for some items usually has the effect of increasing the tax rate on all other activities.

Progressivity—A system under which people with higher incomes must pay more in taxes. This can occur because of a **"graduated rate structure"** that imposes higher statutory (or marginal) tax rates as income rises. Alternatively, the tax code can achieve **"effective progressivity"** by having a large personal exemption. Under the Armey–Shelby flat tax, for instance, a family of four making $30,000 pays no income tax (a zero percent rate), a family of four making $40,000 pays less than 3 percent of their income in taxes, a family of four making $50,000 pays 5.5 percent, and so on until the "effective" rate approaches 17 percent for those with very high incomes (16.94 percent for an income of $10 million).

Savings bias—The double taxation of savings (with some exceptions, such as IRAs) by the current tax system. Income is taxed the year it is earned, and if the taxpayer chooses to save, the interest received is taxed. Income that is consumed, by contrast, escapes additional taxation. There are two ways to alleviate this anti-savings bias: tax-deferred or universal front-ended IRA treatment or yield-exempt, back-ended IRA or municipal bond treatment.

Sixteenth Amendment—An amendment to the U.S. Constitution, ratified more than 80 years ago, which allows the federal government to levy an income tax. Supporters of replacing the income tax with the national sales tax or VAT typically call for its repeal.

Social engineering—Attempts by politicians to steer behavior by granting tax breaks or imposing tax penalties.

Special-interest groups—Groups that seek favoritism in government policy.

Standard deduction—The additional amount of money, similar to the personal exemption and based on filing status, that non-itemizing taxpayers may shield from income.

Supermajority Amendment—A proposed amendment to the U.S. Constitution that would require a two-thirds vote of both the House and Senate to increase taxes (either by raising rates or by expanding the amount of income that is taxable).

Supply-side economics—A school of thought which holds that taxes affect incentives to work, save, invest, and take risks.

Tax base—What is being taxed, or the activity that bears the burden of the tax. How a particular tax reform defines the tax base is one of the most important elements of that reform.

Tax credit—An amount of money that can be deducted directly from a taxpayer's tax liability, and thus is more valuable than a deduction. A $500 credit, for instance, reduces a taxpayer's total bill by $500, while a $500 deduction simply reduces the taxpayer's taxable income by that amount. (For a taxpayer in the 15 percent tax bracket, a $500 deduction produces a tax saving of $75).

Individual retirement account (**IRA**)—Accounts which allow taxpayers to protect savings from double taxation. With traditional IRAs, income that is saved is free from tax, but there is a tax levied on principal and interest when the money is withdrawn (taxing all income only one time). With back-ended (Roth) IRAs, the income is taxed the year it is earned, but there is no second layer of tax on any future interest.

Tax expenditure—Provisions of law granting preferential tax status on the basis of how income is earned or spent. The word "expenditure" is used to highlight the similarity between the use of the tax code to provide advantages to a select group and the more traditional method of giving the group a slice of the federal budget. The proper definition of a tax expenditure, needless to say, would require a proper definition of the tax base.

Tax Limitation Amendment—*See* Supermajority Amendment.

Tax shelter—A loophole in the Internal Revenue Code that people use to lower their tax liability.

Value-added tax (**VAT**)—A form of sales tax under which the tax is levied on the value to a product that is added at each stage of the production process.

Wealth tax—A tax levied on wealth directly, on changes in the value of wealth, or on transfers of wealth. Estate taxes and capital gains taxes are wealth taxes. Assuming that the income used originally to create the wealth has already been taxed, most wealth taxes are examples of double taxation.

SELECTED BIBLIOGRAPHY

Adams, Charles. *For Good and Evil: The Impact of Taxes on the Course of Civilization* (New York: Madison Books, 1993).

American Legislative Exchange Council. *State Revenue and Expenditure Report*, Washington, D.C., July 1990.

Armey, Dick. *The Flat Tax: A Citizen's Guide to the Facts on What It Will Do for You, Your Country, and Your Pocketbook* (New York: Fawcett Columbine, 1996).

—— "Your Tax Return on a Postcard," at *http://flattax.house.gov/welcome.htm*.

Barry, John S. "How a Flat Tax Would Affect Charitable Contributions," Heritage Foundation *Backgrounder* No. 1093, December 16, 1996.

Barry, John S. "New Thoughts on Charitable Donations and Tax Reform," Heritage Foundation *F.Y.I.* No. 135, April 10, 1997.

Bartlett, Bruce. "Don't Cut Taxes—Flatten Them," *Fortune*, April 17, 1995.

Barton, Joe. "The Balanced Budget Amendment: Ending the Federal Spending Binge," Remarks of Representative Joe Barton (R-TX) to The Heritage Foundation, January 5, 1995.

Beach, William W. "The Case for Repealing the Estate Tax," Heritage Foundation *Backgrounder* No. 1091, August 21, 1996.

—— "Why Taxes Affect Economic Growth," Heritage Foundation *Lecture* No. 624, September 24, 1998.

Beach, William W., and Daniel J. Mitchell. "The Flat Tax Cuts Individual Income Taxes in Every State," Heritage Foundation *F.Y.I.* No. 86, February 7, 1996.

—— "Worst Case Scenario: Flat Tax Would Boost Home Values by 7 Percent or More," Heritage Foundation *F.Y.I.* No. 87, February 12, 1996.

Blackwell, J. Kenneth. *Tax Limitation Amendment: Hearings on H.J. Res. 159 Before the Subcommittee on the Constitution of the House Committee on the Judiciary,* 104th Cong., 2nd Sess., 1996.

Bruce, Donald, and Douglas Holtz-Eakin. "Apocalypse Now? Fundamental Tax Reform and Residential Housing Values," National Bureau of Economic Research *Working Paper* No. 6282, November 1997.

Burton, David R., and Dan R. Mastromarco. "Emancipating America from the Income Tax," Cato Institute *Policy Analysis* No. 272, April 15, 1997.

Congressional Budget Office. *For Better or for Worse: Marriage and the Federal Income Tax* (Washington, D.C.: U.S. Government Printing Office, June 1997).

Davis, Shelley. *Unbridled Power: Inside the Secret Culture of the IRS* (New York: Harper Collins Publishers, 1997).

Foster, J. D. *The Flat Tax and Housing Values* (Washington, D.C.: Tax Foundation, 1996).

Furchtgott Roth, Diana, and Christine Stolba. *Women's Figures: The Economic Progress of Women in America* (Washington, D.C.: Independent Women's Forum and the American Enterprise Institute, 1996).

Golob, John E. "How Would Tax Reform Affect Financial Markets?" Federal Reserve Bank of Kansas City *Economic Review,* Fourth Quarter, 1995.

Gravelle, Jane G. *The Flat Tax and Other Proposals: Effects on Housing* (Washington, D.C.: Congressional Research Service, 1996).

Hall, Robert E., and Alvin Rabushka. *The Flat Tax* (Stanford, Cal.: Hoover Institution Press, 1995).

Hayek, F. A. *The Constitution of Liberty* (Chicago: Regnery Publishing, Inc., 1972).

Lindsey, Lawrence B. *The Growth Experiment: How the New Tax Policy Is Transforming the U.S. Economy* (New York: Basic Books, Inc., 1990).

Mathias, William T. "Curtailing the Economic Distortions of the Mortgage Interest Deduction," *University of Michigan Journal of Law Reform*, Fall 1996.

Mitchell, Daniel J. "737,734,941,858 Reasons...and Still Counting: Why a Flat Tax Is Needed to Reform the IRS," Heritage Foundation *Backgrounder* No. 1170, April 15, 1998.

—— "The Case for a Tax Supermajority Requirement: A Look at the States," Citizens for a Sound Economy *Issue Analysis* No. 25, April 12, 1996.

—— *The Flat Tax: Freedom, Fairness, Jobs, and Growth* (Washington, D.C.: Regnery Publishing, Inc., 1996).

—— "Flat Tax or Sales Tax? A Win-Win Choice for America," Heritage Foundation *Backgrounder* No. 1134, August 14, 1997.

—— "A Guide to the Flat Tax: What Everyone In Business Should Know," Heritage Foundation *Backgrounder* No. 1103, February 10, 1997.

—— "How to Fix the Marriage Penalty in the Tax Code," Heritage Foundation *Backgrounder* No. 1250, February 8, 1999.

—— "Jobs, Growth, Freedom and Fairness: Why America Needs a Flat Tax," Heritage Foundation *Backgrounder* No. 1035, May 25, 1995.

—— "Why Liberals Should Support the Flat Tax," Heritage Foundation *F.Y.I.* No. 85, February 7, 1996.

Poterba, James M. "House Price Dynamics: The Role of Tax Policy and Demography," *Brookings Papers on Economic Activity* No. 2, 1991.

Rahn, Richard W. "The New Monetary Universe and Its Impact on Taxation," in James A. Dorn, ed., *The Future of Money in the Information Age* (Washington, D.C.: Cato Institute, 1997).

—— *The End of Money and the Struggle for Financial Privacy* (Seattle, Wash.: Discovery Institute Press, 1999).

Roberts, Paul Craig. *The Supply-Side Revolution* (Cambridge, Mass.: Harvard University Press, 1984).

Shlaes, Amity. *The Greedy Hand: How Taxes Drive Americans Crazy and What to Do About It* (New York: Random House, 1999).

"Unleashing America's Potential," Report of the National Commission on Economic Growth and Tax Reform (New York: St. Martin's Griffin, 1996).

Vedder, Richard K., and Lowell E. Gallaway. *Out of Work: Unemployment and Government in Twentieth-Century America* (New York: Holmes & Meier, 1993).

Williams, Walter, J. Kenneth Blackwell, John Fund, and Steve Forbes. "The Flat Tax: Revitalizing the American Dream," Heritage Foundation *Lecture* No. 569, April 8, 1996.